Fundamental Analysis
for
Financial Markets Traders

by
Jay and Julie Hawk

First edition.

Published by Jellyhawk Financial Press

Copyright © 2018 Jay and Julie Hawk

www.thefxperts.com

All rights reserved. This book or any portion thereof may not be reproduced or used in any manner whatsoever without the express written permission of the authors except for the use of brief quotations in a book review.

ISBN-13: 978-1983784590
ISBN-10: 1983784591

DEDICATION

This book is dedicated to our dear family who loved us, believed in us and encouraged us to excel in our chosen professions

JAY AND JULIE HAWK

FUNDAMENTAL ANALYSIS FOR FINANCIAL MARKETS TRADERS

TABLE OF CONTENTS

	Dedication	iii
	Table of Contents	v
	Acknowledgements	vii
	Foreword	ix
1	Introduction to Fundamental Analysis	Pg #1
2	Foreign Exchange Market Fundamentals	Pg #5
3	Stock Market Fundamentals	Pg #15
4	Commodity Market Fundamentals	Pg #33
5	U.S. Economic Indicators Explained	Pg #47
6	Recommended Further Reading	Pg #69
	About the Authors	Pg #73
	Glossary	Pg #77
	Index	Pg #87

JAY AND JULIE HAWK

ACKNOWLEDGMENTS

This book is the product of many years of personal experience and research obtained by working professionally in the financial markets, trading for our own accounts, and writing about trading as freelancers. We want to thank those who brought us up, those who taught us how to trade, and those who paid us to write for them.

JAY AND JULIE HAWK

FOREWORD

As long term professional experts and authors in the field of financial markets and derivatives trading, one of the most exciting things we have had the opportunity to witness personally in our careers was the electronification of the major financial markets and the advent of online forex and CFD trading for retail speculators.

That important development meant a trader no longer had to be a high-net worth individual, producer, corporation or a market professional to buy and sell currency pairs, stocks or commodities, and they could far more efficiently trade such assets for profit from the convenience of their own homes and even from mobile devices.

Once that market evolution happened, almost anyone could then open up a margin trading account with an online Contract for Difference or CFD broker and trade CFDs speculatively on margin, even if they only had a small stake to put at risk. All they needed was a reasonably modern computer connected to the Internet that they could run an electronic trading platform on.

With relatively sophisticated trading software like MetaTrader available freely as downloadable software and a plethora of online brokers vying for retail business, this just made the financial markets even more accessible to virtually any person who wanted to get involved. This remarkable phenomenon notably changed the formerly structured and highly regulated world of trading dramatically. Now the general public wanted to try their hands at speculating on forex, stock and commodity market movements too!

Over the years since that major financial market evolution occurred, we have been on the forefront of educating the increasingly savvy public about how to trade the various financial markets profitably. Even for many experienced traders, operating successfully in the financial markets can be a challenge due to the inherent volatility of market prices. Inexperienced traders were further hampered by their lack of knowledge about how to trade and analyze the fundamental and technical factors that move market prices.

The harsh reality remains that without a solid foundation, most buildings do not last very long, and the same holds true for financial market traders. Without a solid educational foundation and a good working understanding of how the commodity market operates, how to analyze the markets, and how to make money consistently when trading, the margin accounts of most would-be traders are quickly depleted.

Knowing this all too well, we aimed to use our insider expertise obtained working as professional traders to help such retail traders by writing widely on the subject for numerous Internet websites so that they could freely access this insider information. Working for over a decade as freelance writers, we have at this point contributed thousands of articles to this information pool, as well as online courses, e-books and reports. We even ghostwrote several published books on the subject of financial markets that were attributed to other writers.

With this book, we offer the first in a two-part series of planned books on analyzing the financial markets. In it, we intend to share our knowledge and expertise in fundamental analysis that is deeply relevant to the forex, stock and commodity markets with the public in a different format.

Our goal in publishing a book under our own names is to take a higher-profile role in educating prospective traders realistically about what is involved in trading financial markets profitably and to complement the background of more experienced traders with professional market analysis methods and techniques that they may not yet be familiar with. Successful trading is not exactly easy, but it does not have to be overly difficult either, especially with access to the proper tools and education.

This guide to fundamental analysis is designed to give traders and prospective traders a solid foundation to build upon as they operate in any of the financial markets. We intend to do this by sharing our insider knowledge about the different established fundamental analysis methods relevant for the forex, stock and commodity markets that we are most intimately familiar with. We also provide a handy reference guide to understanding each of the major fundamental U.S. economic indicators, which traders who operate in markets affected by the U.S. economy really need to know about.

The initial chapter of this book introduces the topic of fundamental analysis, discusses various issues with it, and compares it to the technical analysis methods that we cover in the second book in this two-part series. Subsequent chapters deal with how to perform fundamental analysis of the forex, stock and commodity markets, which we treat separately since underlying fundamental factors often differ significantly in their ability to move each of those markets.

These introductory chapters are then followed by a comprehensive reference section covering each of the major U.S. economic indicators that fundamental analysts generally need to be familiar with. We then finish off the book by offering some helpful ideas for further reading that we found very valuable when we were starting our trading education, as well as a bit of information about our professional backgrounds to establish our authority to educate on this subject and a glossary of commonly-used financial terms pertaining to the stock, forex and commodity markets.

While the age-old trading goal of "buying low and selling high" continues to be the key when pursuing a profit in any financial market, having some decent insider knowledge about the principles of fundamental analysis under your belt can really help you better discern what levels are high and what levels are low.

Nevertheless, while traders need to be aware of the fundamental factors covered in this book, they also do not need to overcomplicate their trading decisions by performing excessive amounts of fundamental analysis, especially since many of the most successful trading plans and techniques can be extremely simple. Such simple strategies are also often the most profitable since they are the easiest to apply quickly in a fast moving market, and traders using them can therefore capture more of the anticipated move.

Overall, we think this first book on fundamental analysis in our financial markets analysis series published by Jellyhawk Financial Press will make an excellent introduction to what can appear to be a complicated subject. We do this by highlighting and explaining what you really need to know about the rather broad topic of fundamental analysis, and we intended for this book to educate both novice and seasoned traders alike.

In concluding, we wish our readers great success in their financial trading careers and hope they enjoy them as much as we have ours.

Jay and Julie Hawk
www.thefxperts.com
Northern California, January, 2018

CHAPTER 1: INTRODUCTION TO FUNDAMENTAL ANALYSIS

In order to differentiate pure gambling or speculation from strategic trading, a key element of a typical trading plan will involve analyzing the financial market being traded to determine its most likely future direction. This is done so that positions can be established to profit from an accurate directional prediction.

Fundamental economic indicators are some of the primary types of information reviewed by fundamental analysts. They remain fairly consistent between financial markets and are released periodically by the country they pertain to.

Nevertheless, other relevant fundamental factors can vary considerably between markets. As a result, a fundamental trader needs to know each market's key fundamental price-moving factors in order to understand what shifts the market's direction and why longer term trends and market corrections occur.

Fundamental versus Technical Analysis

The two primary types of market analysis used by traders consist of fundamental and technical analysis. Fundamental analysis takes into account various material and immaterial factors that may affect an asset's market valuation and is generally most relevant to long term price movements, while technical analysis focuses on variations and levels of market observables like price, volume and open interest and helps traders time market entry and exit points.

Since technical analysis focuses largely on an asset's price or exchange rate action and the behavior of other market observables like volume and open interest, as well as on indicators computed from them, using that analytical method can often be reduced to a set of rules that often lends itself well to automation and inclusion into an objective trade plan.

In contrast, fundamental analysis typically requires a human to perform it due to its greater complexity and the need to make judgment calls about the relative importance of various factors and read news and other financial reports.

For these reasons, most traders use fundamental analysis to assess the reasons and causes for long term trends in practice, while also using technical analysis for timing market entry and exit points. This winning combination allows them to add an objective element to their trading plans when it comes to signaling the time to trade, while still grasping the big picture about why market movements are taking place.

Those traders interested in exploring technical analysis further are referred to Volume 2 of this market analysis series for traders written by the same authors and published by Jellyhawk Financial Press in which various technical analysis methods are covered in great detail, along with how to apply them properly in a trading environment.

Before this book covers the particulars of how to perform fundamental analysis for the currency, stock and commodity markets, it first makes sense to review some of the issues with relying solely on fundamental analysis as a financial markets trader.

Issues with Fundamental Analysis

In terms of the point of separation between the two disciplines of technical and fundamental analysis, it has already been noted that technicians rely primarily on price, volume and open interest data, as well as information derived from those market observables, as they evolve over time. Fundamental analysts, on the other hand, take into account just about everything else other than those factors.

Furthermore, when considering the relative merits of focusing on fundamental analysis versus the technical forms of market analysis, many seasoned traders note some serious issues both with the time and lack of objectively involved in performing fundamental analysis and also with its effectiveness as a technique for forecasting near term price moves.

The rest of this section contains a discussion of some of their more common issues seen with applying fundamental analysis to trading the financial markets.

Fundamentals Take Time

When it comes to performing an analysis to obtain a currency forecast, a fundamental analyst usually has to review a far greater set of information than the technical analyst. Since time is money in the financial markets, and trading opportunities can easily be missed if prompt action is not taken, any delay in pulling the trigger on a trade can have a significant adverse impact on your trading business.

For example, a forex fundamental analyst might have to look over a slew of economic data for the country of each currency in a currency pair, plus take into account interest rate, inflation, purchasing power parity, and growth differentials, as well as supply and demand effects, political influences, geopolitical events and relevant commodity prices. Stock and commodity market analysis can get even more involved, since additional things like balance sheets or even weather forecasts will often be reviewed when performing fundamental analysis.

Basically, the task of performing a comprehensive fundamental analysis for a financial market asset can get quite daunting, especially for those without strong analytical training and an economic background. As a result, fundamentals-based traders can easily get left behind and stuck deep in analysis paralysis, while the market technician may have already performed their analysis and moved appropriately into the market in a more timely fashion, and they may even have automated their trading plan entirely.

Lack of Specific Trade Recommendations

Most technical analysts have developed and follow in a disciplined way one or more clearly-defined trade plans. These sets of trading guidelines tell them valuable and objective information about what to look for, when to enter the market, and at what levels positions should be liquidated at a profit or loss. Technical trade plans also usually incorporate money management principles that tell the trader how to size their trades, generally depending on their risk tolerance and portfolio size.

Unfortunately, fundamental analysts usually do not enjoy the advantage of having such clear trade plans. It can be difficult to incorporate all of the information they need to review into a specific trade recommendation with pre-defined entry and exit points. The resulting lack of objectivity can often make the difference between a financial markets trader being successful or not.

All News is Old News

The idea behind this issue with fundamental analysis is that any news released to the public has pretty much already been noted, analyzed and fully discounted into the exchange rate by professional market-makers. Such people specialize in quoting prices in a particular asset and change their prices as soon as news is released to reflect updated valuation information.

Basically, their intense job requires them to keep their fingers right on the pulse of the market using rapid market data services, news wires and the market's own well-developed rumor-mill. Large traders might even establish directional positions ahead of the fact to profit from expected movements based on rumors, large anticipated transactions or their own in-house valuation analysis.

As a result, traders looking to take positions based on fundamentals will often be sorely frustrated to see the market react to news in a thoroughly counter-intuitive way as the market pros "buy the rumor and sell the fact."

CHAPTER 2: FOREIGN EXCHANGE MARKET FUNDAMENTALS

When it comes to foreign exchange or forex trading, fundamental analysis generally involves going over the economic indicators, government fiscal policies, social and political factors, and interest rates of one country and comparing them to the corresponding factors of another country. This allows forex traders to get a sense of how one country's currency should be valued relative to that of another and how such relative valuations may shift in future.

Fundamental analysis uses such information as a way of forecasting foreign exchange rate trends. While this technique commonly appeals to those traders with an education in economics, just about anyone can learn to determine what fundamental factors move the forex market.

Furthermore, since currency exchange rates represent the equilibrium balance point between supply and demand in the base currency against the counter-currency, the resulting exchange rate reflects not an absolute value, but instead the relative strength or weakness of these currencies against one another. As a result, fundamental data for each currency is required to make an attempt to predict directional movements for the currency pair.

The rest of this section will describe the basics of fundamental analysis and how to use its techniques to trade forex.

Key Fundamental Economic Data

The release dates of key economic numbers are widely tabulated in economic calendars and can involve considerable market volatility if the actual number released differs significantly from the market's consensus.

The list below includes most of the key economic data releases that reporting agencies within the various countries provide to the market on a regular basis as indicated.

- **Employment Data** – Released monthly
- **Gross Domestic Product (GDP)** – Released quarterly
- **Trade Balance** – Released monthly
- **Retail Sales** – Released monthly
- **Industrial Production** – Released monthly
- **Consumer Price Index (CPI)** – Released monthly
- **Producer Price Index (PPI)** – Released monthly.

Other Types of Fundamental Information

In addition to the aforementioned economic data, some of the other important fundamental information commonly used by traders and economists in performing fundamental analysis might include the following:

- Differences in interest rates
- Supply and demand effects
- Political influences
- Geopolitical events
- Growth rate differentials
- Commodity prices
- Survey results
- The Commitment of Traders or COT positioning reports.

Using Fundamentals to Trade Forex

When performing a fundamental analysis on a particular currency pair, forex traders will look at as many fundamental factors as possible for the countries of the currencies they wish to forecast, and they will take this data into account relative to one another.

Traders do this in order to obtain a broad sense of what each country's economic, growth and political climate is. This method is similar to how stock analysts might review data for corporations they are considering making recommendations about.

Basically, if the data looks better for the base currency's country relative to the counter currency's country, then that would tend to imply a rising forecast for their exchange rate. On the other hand, if the base currency's country's data comes across as weaker, then a falling forecast would tend to ensue for the relevant exchange rate. A neutral forecast would apply when prospects are roughly the same on balance for the two countries.

Once having made such a forecast, the fundamental currency trader would then position themselves in the forex market to take advantage of the forecast movements in the exchange rate. Over time, they would update this analysis as news events and data releases occur, and would adjust their trading positions accordingly.

Currency Valuation Factors

The worth or value of a currency in the forex market is generally expressed in relative rather than absolute terms. Accordingly, the value of the currency of each nation will be quoted relative to that of the currencies of other nations in currency pairs. Furthermore, this market valuation responds sensitively to long-term economic and interest rate cycles.

Although economic theorists might postulate that forex market rate fluctuations form an essentially random walk through time, and some even use this hypothetical assumption when developing theoretical currency option pricing models, for example, almost any cursory review of a chart of a currency pair's exchange rate plotted over time will probably convince you otherwise.

Basically, forex rates often show remarkable tendencies to trend in a particular direction over time, often as a response to underlying interest rate adjustments by the relevant central banks.

Furthermore, the repeatability of the aggregate behavior of large groups of humans often reflects itself in the formation of recognizable technical price patterns that set up reliable outcomes. As detailed in the previous section on technical analysis, many technical forex traders use such patterns to forecast future exchange rate movements.

Currencies Seen as the Stock of a Nation

Another way to look at forex valuation is that a currency's value behaves as if it were the stock of a nation. If a corporation is doing well and giving good dividends, then its stock tends to rise. Likewise, if a nation is doing well economically and its interest rates are either attractive to investors or tending to become more so, then the currency of that nation will tend to strengthen relative to currencies of nations with less buoyant economies and lower or declining interest rates.

Naturally, this valuation analogy requires something of an oversimplification of the situation, especially given the global nature of the marketplace and the complex interaction of supply and demand effects. Nevertheless, this comparison can provide a simple framework within which to understand how the forex market values currencies.

Currency Valuation Factors

Many forex experts would agree that the main factor in currency valuation involves the interest rate differential between the currency pair in question. Nevertheless, additional currency valuation factors can include such things as:

- Economic growth prospects.
- Inflation rate and forecasts.
- Trade deficits or surpluses.
- The nation's money supply.
- What type of security or credit quality the country uses to back its currency.

The Effect of Currency Reserves on Valuation

Sometimes, a particular currency will be treated as a reserve currency and be held by central banks and financial institutions to pay international debts with or used to intervene in the currency market to support their currency with.

The U.S. Dollar has historically been used extensively for this purpose, as well as for the buying and selling of key commodities like oil and gold. As a result of this traditional usage for Dollars, the currency often remains strong despite an economic downturn or other financial problems in the United States.

Central banks also often keep reserves of other major currencies, and the size of these reserves determines how much of a war chest they have available to defend their own currency with, just in case it comes under severe selling pressure.

All of the aforementioned currency valuation factors will tend to have an effect on the exchange rate of the various currency pairs, to a greater or lesser extent. As a result, it pays to keep an eye on the fundamental economic picture of the countries involved since it can be a helpful indicator when it comes to forecasting the long-term behavior of one currency's valuation relative to that of another.

How Interest Rate Changes Affect the Forex Market

Interest rates consist of perhaps the most significant determinant of foreign exchange rates. Furthermore, when it comes to considering how interest rate levels and their changes tend to affect the forex market, economic analysts generally look not at the real interest rate prevailing in a country, but instead at the nominal or benchmark interest rate set by a country's central bank.

In practice, forex rates usually trend over the medium and longer term to favor the currency with the higher nominal interest rate. Furthermore, central banks set benchmark nominal interest rates to reflect their stance on monetary policy.

As a result, hawkish statements from monetary policymakers indicating higher nominal interest rates for the country tend to benefit its currency well in advance of any actual movements seen in nominal interest rates.

The rest of this section discusses how interest rate changes can affect currency valuations in the forex market, including the concept of interest rate parity, how interest rate differentials affect the fundamental prospects for exchange rates, and how forex carry trades take advantage of this.

Interest Rate Parity

Another useful concept involving the relationship between interest rates and foreign exchange rates is known as interest rate parity. This idea basically postulates the equality of fully-hedged returns obtained from making investments in different currencies.

This means that such returns would not depend on the actual levels of interest rates seen in the different currencies. This parity concept generally requires efficient international markets with no barriers to investment flows to hold true.

Interest Rate Differentials

As the name implies, the interest rate differential between a currency pair is readily determined by taking the difference between the interest rate prevailing in the first currency's country and the interest rate seen in the second currency's country.

If each country is perceived as sufficiently safe for investment, international capital flows soon move in to take advantage of any such differential by seeking to make deposits at the higher rate. To do so, managers of such fluid funds first need to purchase the higher-rate currency, and so demand for that currency gradually increases. Eventually, this will result in that currency's appreciation against the lower-rate currency.

Since interest rate differentials are used to price foreign exchange forward outrights, currency futures and forward swaps, in addition to European-style currency options, any changes in these differentials will impact not just the pricing seen in the spot market for affected currency pairs, but also the forex forward and option markets.

Interest Rate Parity

The concept of interest rate parity refers to the relationship between foreign exchange rates and interest rates. The fundamental tenet of interest rate parity requires that hedged returns from investments made in differing currencies should be equal, irrespective of the actual levels of their respective interest rates.

Interest rate differentials provide the pricing basis for foreign exchange forward swaps and forward outrights, as well as contributing to the theoretical valuation of European-style currency options. Also, they can be readily exploited by forex traders willing to engage in the increasingly popular pursuit of foreign exchange carry trades.

Carry Trades

Interest rate changes also affect the attractiveness of carry trades involving the currency for which the interest rate has changed. Basically, carry trades involve borrowing in a low interest rate currency to invest in assets denominated in a higher interest rate currency in the hopes of capturing the interest rate differential. Such trades generally involve taking foreign exchange risk.

Carry trades can be done via the forex market by entering into a forward outright contract to buy the high interest rate currency and sell the low interest rate currency. Such a contract will usually be priced at a discount relative to the current spot rate to account for the interest rate differential.

If the spot rate does not move, gains will gradually accumulate on this position over time. Eventually, the carry trader wants the spot rate to end up at a level worse than the rate on the forward contract when it is two business days from delivery so that they can close out the contract for a profit.

Implementing Forex Carry Trades

Perhaps the simplest way for a forex trader to get into a carry trade would be to sell a lower interest rate currency and buy a higher interest rate currency forward for the desired time frame of the carry trade.

Nevertheless, other ways of implementing carry trades exist for those willing to enter into transactions outside of the forex market. For example, such a carry trader might elect to borrow in the lower interest rate currency and then invest the proceeds of the loan in government-backed securities in a currency with a higher interest rate.

Carry Trade Example in AUD/JPY

Due to the exceptionally low interest rates seen in Japan during recent years as the country has struggled with low growth and deflationary pressures, the Japanese Yen has been involved in numerous foreign exchange carry trades as the short or borrowed currency.

On the other hand, Australia has enjoyed a period of relative economic strength compared to other major economies which has kept its interests rates relatively high and on a currently-increasing trend. These factors, along with Australia's notable political stability and the added benefit the country receives from recent higher prices for its gold exports, have made the Australian Dollar a relatively safe and lucrative place to invest funds in carry trades.

Accordingly, a presently-attractive carry trade would involve borrowing Japanese Yen and lending Australian Dollars. A forex trader could implement a carry trade in this currency pair by buying AUD/JPY as a forward outright contract at a rate substantially below the current spot rate due to the substantial interest rate differential favoring the AUD.

The trader might then hold the position patiently, as it picked up value from the interest rate differential every day. Once the trader's forward contract is two business days from delivery, if the AUD/JPY spot rate is not trading below the initial outright rate on the contract, the transaction will earn a profit for the trader.

The Effect of Purchasing Power Parity on Exchange Rates

The quantity of a particular basket of basic goods which can be purchased in a certain country with the money produced by that country is known as Purchasing Power Parity or PPP. Parity can be determined by knowing what the same basket of goods would cost in each country under consideration.

For example, the United States generally acts as the PPP standard, and it could therefore be given a value of 100. Bermuda, having a PPP value of 154 on this scale, has the highest PPP in the world. The PPP number of 154 implies that goods in Bermuda cost 54% more than what the same goods typically cost in the United States.

The rest of this section will discuss what purchasing power parity is and the effects it has on exchange rates seen in the forex market.

Purchasing Power Parity and Its Implications

Since Purchasing Power Parity or PPP measures the relative purchasing power of two currencies, it remains a very important concept for fundamental forex traders to grasp. PPP also forms the basis of many trade plans that use fundamental factors to assess the future direction of forex rates.

As an example of what Purchasing Power Parity means to the foreign exchange market, if it were to prevail, the exchange rate between two countries would theoretically equal the ratio of what would be paid in each country for a fixed basket of goods and services. That implies a particular exchange rate, so if the observed market rate deviates significantly from that PPP exchange rate, then it could be expected to trend closer to that ideal level over time.

Furthermore, if one of the two relevant countries is experiencing high inflation, where domestic prices for goods are rising notably, then the currency of that country would depreciate in order for the exchange rate to eventually return to Purchasing Power Parity.

The Law of One Price

In economics, the Law of One Price states that "in an efficient market, all identical goods must have only one price." As an example of this, suppose that a desirable car can be purchased in Canada for $15,000 Canadian Dollars. The same car costs $10,000 in the United States, so the implied USD/CAD exchange rate would be 1.5 Canadian Dollars to 1 U.S. Dollar.

Nevertheless, if the same car began selling in Canada for 12,000 Canadian Dollars, then people from the United States would probably flock to nearby Canada to buy the car once that opportunity became known, and with all other factors remaining equal.

The price ratio of the car to the currency would imply that the Canadian Dollar was then worth 1.2 to 1 U.S. Dollar, so the USD/CAD exchange rate would theoretically depreciate to that level if this happened on a larger scale.

PPP and Currency Valuation

Obviously, Purchasing Power Parity should have considerable importance in the relative valuation of currencies and can even affect the economic prospects of entire nations. Generally, countries where wages are low will have a lower standard of living and a lower cost of goods.

The PPP number for such a country would be under 100, which is the number corresponding to the United States. Canada and Australia both have a PPP number of 90, meaning that goods and services in these two countries cost roughly 10% less than the equivalent goods and services in the United States.

Sustained Divergences from PPP

Although PPP takes the cost of living and inflation into account, some major differences exist between the PPP and exchange rates in some instances. China for example has a PPP of 1.8 Chinese Yuan to 1 U.S. Dollar. Nevertheless, the actual Yuan/Dollar exchange rate is 7.5 Yuan to the Dollar.

This means that the Yuan in China actually buys almost five times more goods and services than the Dollar in the United States. The Yuan represents a classic case of a PPP divergence sustained by an intentional undervaluation of a currency by its issuing country.

Accordingly, Purchasing Power Parity indirectly affects currency exchange rates through its influence on commodity prices and the economic growth rate of each country. Where large discrepancies exist, arbitrage through commodity purchases is possible, and this tends to eventually bring exchange rates back toward parity over time.

CHAPTER 3: STOCK MARKET FUNDAMENTALS

Those performing fundamental analysis for stocks often look at the relative economic and political status of the country and industry that a stock issuer is operating in versus another. Stock fundamental analysis also typically involves performing a detailed corporate analysis, including reviewing dividends, debt to equity ratios, operating margins, stock buyback and issuance programs, and overall business performance.

Furthermore, most fundamental stock analysts will review a company's latest balance sheet for various factors to determine how strong the firm looks relative to others in its market sector and to assess whether or not its stock seems cheap or expensive based on its assets versus liabilities.

The following sections will further explain fundamental elements involved in trading and investing in stocks, as well as the various techniques and indicators used to perform fundamental analysis for stocks.

Trading Stocks

In order to trade stocks, getting some basic fundamental knowledge about stocks and how they trade before putting money at risk can be extremely beneficial to the novice. Knowing the nature of stocks and their role in the world of investing and finance can be invaluable to anyone considering investing or trading in the stock market.

The rest of this section discusses key fundamental elements of stock trading and what people need to know in order to trade stocks, which generally involves strategic speculation, so has more in common with gambling than with investing for long term capital appreciation.

The Stock Market and Why Stocks are Important

Basically, a stock represents an ownership right to a corporation. This contrasts to a bond which is a debt instrument issued to a creditor of a corporation. Furthermore, stock owners are subordinate to bond owners in the priority of a corporation's financing.

Why do companies issue stock? Companies issue and trade stocks for a variety of reasons. One of the main reasons has to do with spreading the risk of ownership, and another important motivation involves financing the expansion of the corporation.

Example of a Corporation Issuing Stock

When corporations are formed, the government requires that they have a corporate charter. In it, the corporation needs to state the intentions of the corporation and how much stock in the corporation exists. The charter also names the main stockholders of the corporation, who would consist of the initial owners of the corporation.

The corporation's charter will typically carry provisions for the issuing of stock to the public if the company decides to become a publicly-traded company. Otherwise, the company can remain private with the shares of the company's stock remaining in private hands. The stock of the corporation can also be offered to outside parties through a private transaction.

Stocks trading in this manner are typically transacted between parties privately without the need of a centralized exchange. Basically, the company remains private and the transaction occurs between the corporation and an individual investor, for example.

Issuing Stock to the Public

When a corporation decides it needs a large influx of capital to expand operations, or has determined that spreading the risk of the original investment was in the best interests of the original stockholders, the corporation can choose to take the company public.

Most corporations include clauses in their charter for this eventuality, with a pre-determined amount of stock set aside for issuance in the event of an Initial Public Offering or IPO. When the time for an IPO comes, the corporation will require the services of an investment banker to determine a fair price and to distribute the newly-issued stock to the public.

The corporation may also issue more than one type of stock, such as "preferred stock." In addition, stock trading often begins privately before the new stocks are offered to the general public.

Listed and Unlisted Stocks

Listed stocks refer to stocks trading on a centralized stock exchange such as the New York Stock Exchange or NYSE. Unlisted stocks are not listed on an exchange and generally trade over a network. The latter are considered "Over-The-Counter" or OTC stocks.

Interestingly, OTC stocks include some big corporate names like Microsoft and Sun Microsystems. Both of these corporations have preferred to continue trading on the OTC market, despite the prestige associated with NYSE-traded companies.

While stocks trading OTC offer investors the advantage of not paying exchange fees, the lack of a centralized trading location can make for increased volatility.

Basically, trading in stocks, commodities or currencies in most cases involves pure speculation on price or exchange-rate fluctuations. On the other hand, those who invest in stocks will often be making a longer-term investment in a company's future with the goal of capital appreciation as the next section will discuss.

Investing in Stocks

While trading is more of a speculative pursuit somewhat akin to strategic gambling, investing generally involves placing money into an asset or venture with the objective of earning long term gains.

A number of reasons exist for an investor to want to invest their money in stocks, and one of the more common motivations is that stock investments have a history of outperforming many other investments over a long period of time.

A growing segment of the population now invests in the stock market to maximize their money's overall return and to protect the value of their money against inflation.

While trading in the forex and commodities markets generally takes on a more speculative nature, stocks can make extremely profitable investments over a longer time frame, depending on which ones are chosen, of course. In addition, some stocks pay out quarterly dividends which give people even more incentive to invest in stocks.

The rest of this section discusses how stock investments have traditionally been made to hedge against inflation, what fundamental factors are taken into account when picking stocks, and why it pays to invest in stocks.

Obtain Diversity in the Stock Market

A key principle in money management involves the principle of diversification, and having different types of stocks in your investment portfolio can help prevent issues associated with putting all your financial eggs into one basket. Basically, by diversifying one's portfolio and investing in a variety of different sectors of the economy, the investor stands a much better chance of achieving consistently above-average returns.

The stock market represents the sum total of all publicly-traded corporations which are involved in virtually all sectors of economic activity. By choosing the right stock investments, an investor can indirectly take a gold position, for example, which they could do by purchasing shares in a gold mine.

Furthermore, perhaps an investor's goals are to earn a competitive rate of return without taking too much risk on a stock. In this case, they might consider investing in electric utilities which have traditionally traded for low dollar amounts, pay out large dividends, trade at low price/earnings multiples, and generally offer investors a high degree of security.

Conversely, an investor might prefer to invest in stocks which have a higher degree of risk, due to greater chances of sharp price fluctuations, since they might desire the possibility of a higher return. If so, a great many choices exist in start-ups and other companies that have prices which are more volatile in nature, of which some Internet stocks can present good examples.

Fundamental Criteria for Choosing Stocks for Investments

Many people who invest in stocks want to be in on the bottom. For example, Microsoft shares have appreciated considerably in price since being originally sold in the 1980's, returning in excess of 60,000 percent from those early days. Innovation and market forces also often play a major role in the price of a stock.

Nevertheless, some basic fundamental elements are usually taken into account when making investments in stocks. These include such key stock valuations factors as:

- **Earnings** - Fund managers, investment bankers and other financial experts evaluate stocks primarily on earnings. If a company is performing well, their earnings will reflect this, and in many cases will cause the price of the stock to rise.

- **Capitalization** – the amount of stock issued by the company can impact the price of the stock considerably, especially if the bulk of outstanding stock is in the hands of just a few shareholders or financial institutions.

- **Debt** – the amount of money the company owes and the terms of their corporate bonds will also have an impact on the price of the stock.

- **Insiders** – certain corporate figures within the company will often invest in stocks from their company, as will investment banks and other institutional traders. Knowing who owns how much stock and whether they are increasing or decreasing their holdings can affect the stock price.

Many stock investors are wondering which stock will be the next Apple Inc. or the next Google. Taking your best guess about this after performing your fundamental research is one of the basic tasks involved in long term stock investing.

The Valuation of Stocks

An important component of the fundamental analysis of stocks consists of the accurate valuation of a company and its stock. The valuation of a company and its stock can give significant clues as to the future price of the stock, and whether the company is undervalued or overvalued.

The use of fundamental data in the analysis of a company's stock gives the analyst an idea of the intrinsic value of the stock, which takes into account the company's assets and its present and future cash flow. While the determination of the value of a company's assets and its present cash flow can indicate the worth of its stock, an accurate valuation may include many intangible factors.

Fundamentals Used to Determine Fair Value

Analysts have traditionally used a number of fundamental factors to determine a stock's "fair value". In addition to the pricing of a company's assets, the fundamental criteria that most impacts a stock's valuation are listed below:

- **Growth Rate** – the expected growth rate of a company carries considerable weight in a stock's valuation. Analyzing the growth rate generally begins by examining historical growth and includes sales growth and income. The Growth Rate can give an accurate indication of whether the company is on the upswing or in decline.

- **Earnings per Share or EPS** – the EPS of a company is determined by taking net annual income and dividing the figure by the number of shares outstanding. Analysts examine two types of EPS: Pro Forma EPS, which excludes any one-time and other non-cash items; and GAAP EPS, which stands for Generally Accepted Accounting Principles and uses the GAAP standard.

- **Price/Earnings Ratio or PE** – the price of the stock divided by the annual amount of earnings. For example, if XYZ stock is trading at $100 per share, and has annual earnings of $10 per share, then the PE for that stock would be 10 ($100 share price/$10 annual earnings=10).

- **Price Earnings to Growth Ratio or PEG** – this fundamental valuation technique takes the price of the stock, the company's annual earnings and the earnings growth rate, which gives the analyst a ratio figure expressed as a percentage. Theoretically, if the percentage is over 100, then the stock is getting overvalued, while a PEG declining below 100% would indicate that the stock is becoming more undervalued.

- **Market Capitalization** – the total value of all of a company's outstanding stock. Market cap is computed by multiplying the stock's current price by the amount of fully diluted shares outstanding.

- **Price to Sales Ratio** – the ratio of the stock's prevailing market price over the amount of cash earned in sales.

- **Return on Investment Capital or ROIC** – the return on the amount of money invested by shareholders and bondholders. The number is generally expressed as a percentage and is determined by taking the net income and dividing the figure by the invested capital, long and short term debt and accounts payable and subsequently subtracting cash on hand and accounts receivable.

- **Return on Assets or ROA** – also expressed as a percentage, ROA is similar to ROIC and measures a company's capability to make money from its assets. This figure is determined by taking net income and dividing the figure by the company's total assets.

- **Enterprise Value** – this is the total net worth of the company as represented by the company's stock price. The figure is determined by taking the company's market capitalization and the total net debt, subtracting accounts receivable and cash on hand. The Enterprise value is the closest valuation of the worth of a company.

What Cause Stock Prices to Change?

Understanding the stock market and what makes a stock's price change is essential if you plan to invest in stocks or wish to understand the workings of modern corporate economics. Many factors influence stock prices, some attributable to the overall stock market, while others having to do directly with the business and industry of the underlying corporation.

The rest of this section describes the various fundamental factors that can change a stock's price, both in the initial public offering and the subsequently as it trades in the secondary market.

The Initial Public Offering or IPO

The initial public offering date could be considered the most important day in the life of a stock. The IPO date generally refers to the first day on which the stock will begin trading publicly, either on a stock exchange or on a closed network like the Nasdaq over-the-counter market.

The stock's price can display significant movements on that important day. While it may stabilize shortly thereafter, the stock price will be affected as the market's expectations for the company's business prospects fluctuate over time.

Stock Price Factors after the IPO

After the IPO, the stock trades freely until it finds an appropriate price level based on the supply and demand in the market. Many factors make up the pricing of a stock. These might include the capitalization, or the amount of stock issued versus the assets and liabilities of the company, as well as the past and future performance of the company in its particular business.

The price of some stocks can be commodity-sensitive, such as a gold mining stock or an oil company. Other stock prices, like those of Intel and Microsoft, tend to move as their corporation's technological innovations and successes become factored into their stock's price.

Furthermore, as a corporation's profits improve, its stock price will appreciate in most cases. This gives its shareholders a profit on their original investment. Conversely, if the corporation's profits fail to meet market expectations or the corporation posts unexpected losses, the price of the stock will generally fall and its investors will be disappointed.

General Market Factors

The stock market's cycle also directly impacts stock prices. If a broad bear market in stocks is underway, even stocks of companies that have a high intrinsic value and are continuing to produce earnings, are sold mercilessly. This can create excellent buying opportunities.

Conversely, in bull markets even stocks of companies that are not doing well will tend to rise due to the speculative psychological nature of the masses during a bull market.

Another important factor to consider is the industry of the company, as well as its competitors and how their stocks are performing. Often stocks that make up an important part of an economic or commodity sector will rise and fall in tandem, as is the case with gold-mining stocks.

Dividends

Many companies of older and more established stocks pay dividends to their investors. These dividends can be paid quarterly or bi-annually, depending on the company, but most companies pay out dividends on a quarterly basis.

When a company pays a dividend, the amount of the dividend is taken off of the opening price of the stock on the ex-dividend date. Also, in order to receive the dividend, the stock must be held on the "day of record" which typically falls two days after the ex-dividend date. The amount of the dividend is paid out on the dividend date which comes soon after the day of record.

While dividends may affect the stock price initially, they then do not usually have much effect on the stock price. Exceptions arise when a new dividend is announced, or a company has suspended payment of its dividend for one reason or another. Since dividends can comprise a very important aspect of stock fundamental analysis, they will be discussed further on in this chapter in their own dedicated section.

Stock Price Forecasting

When discussing the fundamental analysis of a company's stock price, one must be aware that the stock price is a function of the public's perception of that company, and that the price of the stock could reflect speculation on how well the company could perform in the distant future versus the present. Other factors may also be involved in the valuation of a stock, such as interest by other parties in acquiring the company or a new product the company may be set to release.

In order to forecast a stock's price in the future, a study of the factors that affect the company's stock price, including revenue and growth, would probably be the most reliable way to determine the stock price's possible future trajectory. Revenue and growth directly impact a company's earnings, therefore they are two of the key elements fundamental analysts use in calculating a company's earnings and the prospects for its stock.

Nevertheless, revenue and growth factors, as well as their determination, depend on the accuracy of the data sets and do not take into account other factors.

Revenue

To make a forecast of a company's revenue, the fundamental analyst would first gather information from the company, the consumers of the company's products and the overall health of the industry. This can be determined from the company's own analysis, as well as from industry trade groups that publish information on market demographics, competing companies and the current market share of the company within the industry.

The company's product then needs to be analyzed, with a study on the different manufacturers of the same product, how competitive the field is and how the company's product compares to its competition. In the case of a service, a thorough evaluation of the cost of doing business and how the service compares to its competitors would give an idea of the company's revenue.

Consumer information can be gleaned from data obtained from surveys and actual product sales. Other data such as the company's financial statement, their inventory and shipments and the number of units of their product expected to sell in the period, give an analyst a perspective on what the current and future prospects for the company's revenue would be.

Growth

Once the analyst has forecast the company's revenue, they can then project future growth. By determining the growth on revenue, the analyst can estimate the company's future earnings. Growth rate projections depend on a variety of factors that include, the product's market share, its price per unit, the industry outlook and the company's prospects in new and existing markets.

While the analyst may make a somewhat accurate forecast of the company's earnings, the prevailing market price of the stock could depend on many other factors including, stock repurchase programs, the release of new products, secondary stock offerings, dividends and stock splits to name just a few.

Ultimately, the market decides on the price of any given stock at any time. In a bull market, even companies with lower expectations rise in value, while in a bear market, good companies with healthy earnings tend to decline in value along with the rest of the market. Therefore, in using fundamental analysis the trader must also be aware of macroeconomic trends that could affect the accuracy of their forecasts.

Mergers and Acquisitions

Mergers and Acquisitions or M&As make up a very important fundamental aspect of corporate finance. As the name implies, a merger is when a company combines or merges with another to form a larger company, while an acquisition is when a corporation bids on and purchases another corporation.

While the two actions may seem similar, the merger consolidates the two companies into one combining the two companies' assets and stock, while in an acquisition, one company takes ownership of the other company's assets, stock, debt and equity interests. In both actions the two companies wind up with shared assets and liabilities.

Difference between a Merger and an Acquisition

Fundamental analysts need to understand the differences between mergers and acquisitions. A basic discussion of each type of corporate consolidation follows.

- *Acquisitions* - Basically, an acquisition is defined as an action in which one corporation proceeds to purchase all or a controlling interest of another company, clearly establishing ownership of the target company. Legally, the targeted company no longer exists, its stock is delisted from trading, while the acquiring company keeps doing business and their stock continues trading.

    An acquisition can be made with cash, stock or a combination of both. In smaller acquisitions, one strategy involves one company purchasing all of the assets of the other company, leaving the targeted firm with only cash, and possibly debt. The targeted firm would then become a shell company that would eventually close down or enter into another business.

    Acquisitions generally fall into two categories: a solicited or friendly acquisition, and an unsolicited or hostile takeover. The friendly takeover has many similarities to a merger and is done with the co-operation of the target company. In a hostile takeover, however, the target company has not agreed to be acquired and the acquiring company has taken steps to a gain a majority ownership through purchasing the target company's stock and/or assets.

- *Mergers* - A merger generally takes place between two similarly sized companies that have agreed to continue doing business as a single entity instead of as two separately owned and operated corporate units. This type of merger is often referred to as a merger of equals, with both companies' stock ceasing to trade separately with a new stock subsequently issued that includes both companies.

An example of a merged company is ExxonMobil. In 1999, the two companies, Exxon and Mobil agreed to merge in an $81 billion deal. Nevertheless, the merger was more of a reunion, since the two companies were both owned by John D. Rockefeller before the Standard Oil Trust was broken up in 1911. Exxon was formally Standard Oil Co. of New Jersey, while Mobil was formally Standard Oil Co. of New York.

Benefits of Combining Two Companies

In the world of mergers and acquisitions, the word "synergy" is often used to describe increased savings, revenue enhancement and cost efficiencies achieved after combining two companies. After becoming one firm the two companies generally benefit from:

- *New Technology* – one of the best reasons for a company to acquire or merge with another is to access new technology, which would make the combined company more competitive.

- *Reductions in Staff* – as is often the case, when two companies combine, the number of staff is reduced. The staff cuts would include the accounting, marketing, sales and other units of one of the companies since only one department would be needed.

- *Market Reach and Access* - one of the most important reasons that companies merge or purchase other companies is that it can vastly improve a company's market reach and visibility. The combination of two companies can enhance both companies' marketing, sales and distribution channels allowing for new growth opportunities. In addition, raising capital can be easier for larger companies versus smaller ones.

How Hostile Takeovers Affect Stock Prices

One of the most unpredictable situations that arise in the fundamental analysis of stocks consists of the hostile takeover of one company by another. A hostile takeover takes place when a company actively purchases another company against the wishes of the target company's board of directors. Stock prices during hostile takeover situations can often be unpredictable, since bids can be accepted the target company, or withdrawn by the aggressor.

Typically, a company subjected to a hostile takeover has vulnerabilities, which can be taken advantage of by the pursuing company, or by a third party. The target company's board of directors could accept or refuse a third party's bid; however, the aggressor party could begin accumulating the target company's stock. The aggressor company's accumulation of the target company's stock could eventually achieve a majority of shares, therefore, giving the aggressor the possibility of forcing the takeover.

Target Company's Stock Behavior

Typically, when a company is targeted for a hostile takeover, the company's stock price begins to appreciate. The aggressor company does not have to disclose their plans immediately, and can often quietly accumulate a stake in the target company's stock before any announcement is made. Nevertheless, once a certain number of shares have been purchased, the aggressor company must disclose its stake to a regulating body such as the Securities and Exchange Commission or SEC in the United States.

When the takeover is announced by the hostile company, they would typically make a tender offer directly to the target company's shareholders at the price that they are willing to pay. The tender price is often significantly higher than the prevailing market share price.

At this point, shareholders willing to part with their shares at the tender offer's price, sell their shares directly to the aggressor company, which sometimes creates arbitrage opportunities. If the shares are offered o an exchange for less than the tender price, an arbitrageur can purchase the shares on the exchange and immediately tender them to the acquiring firm.

While this is occurring, the stock price of the target company gravitates to the tender price. Nevertheless, a risk of the deal falling through may keep shares just under the tender price.

Poison Pills and Greenmail

If the target company's board is against a hostile takeover, they can take measures to discourage the buyer, such as merging with another company or buying back the firm's own stock for example. These measures taken by a targeted company to avoid a takeover are known as "poison pills".

Also, the term "greenmail" refers to the money an aggressor receives after buying a large voting stake in a corporation that they then threaten with a hostile takeover unless the target company repurchases their stake at a higher price to stop the aggressive investor's takeover bid.

Much like the use of the word blackmail, the payment the investor receives is called greenmail. Since 1987, greenmail profits have been subject to a 50% tax in the United States to deter this type of aggressive activity against corporations.

Aggressor Company's Stock Behavior

Typically, the company that is in the process of bidding for another company has a number of capital considerations that put pressure on their stock. The most prominent is obtaining the funds to acquire the target company. If the aggressor company has a large cash reserve, then a cash offer could be advanced; however, if the company is short of cash on hand, then an offer of stock or a combination of cash and stock could be viable.

Regardless of how the company plans to pay for the acquisition, the result generally puts pressure on the aggressor company's stock price. Once the hostile takeover is successful, then the aggressor company's stock tends to recover and its stock price appreciates.

Hostile takeovers also tend to affect the stock prices of companies that compete with the target company and others stocks of companies in related businesses. When takeovers start occurring in a particular business sector, public interest in that sector tends to increase due to media activity, thereby typically driving stock prices in that sector higher.

Dividends

Dividends represent payments made by corporations to their stockholders. These payments generally get paid by companies in either cash, called "cash dividends" or in stock, known as "stock dividends". Not all companies pay out dividends and those that do can change their policy or cancel paying out dividends altogether.

Corporations first raise money by issuing stock, and they then use the proceeds to expand the company. Once the company's growth and earnings have achieved a certain level, the company can then choose to distribute some of their earnings through a cash or stock dividend payment to its shareholders.

Dividends have been paid out to shareholders by companies for over 400 years and are the primary method for corporations to return value to shareholders for investing in their company. Stocks that pay dividends typically outperform both the market and non-dividend paying stocks.

Cash Dividends

Most dividend paying companies structure their dividends around their earnings level and distribute dividends to shareholders every quarter. A stock that distributes a quarterly dividend has what is known as a "dividend yield", which means that the stock will yield an annual percentage amount based on the amount of the dividend.

Nevertheless, some companies schedule their dividend payments bi-annually, annually, while some companies pay out dividends monthly. On occasion, some corporations pay out a one-time special dividend, which is not factored into the dividend yield of the stock.

In order to receive a dividend, shareholders must be "holders of record" which means that they own the stock on the "date of record". The date of record generally ranges from a week to one month before the "ex-dividend" date or the day that the company distributes the dividend to its stockholders.

The cash dividend amount then appears in the shareholder's trading account on the ex-dividend date. If the shareholder bought the stock after the date of record, then they would not be entitled to the dividend. Short sellers of a stock going ex-dividend must pay the dividend amount for each short share.

Stock Dividends

In addition to dividends in the form of cash distributions, some corporations make dividend payments by distributing additional shares of the company's stock to existing shareholders in lieu of a cash dividend. Companies often opt for this type of dividend when their liquid cash reserves are low or their capital is allocated elsewhere.

A stock dividend is typically quoted as a fraction of existing shares, for example, a stock dividend of five percent would give the stockholder an additional five shares for every one hundred shares owned, or one share for every 20 shares owned. Stock dividends have a tax advantage, since they are not taxed until the newly distributed shares are sold.

While not immediately apparent, a stock dividend dilutes the value of existing shares by the percentage of the dividend. For example, if the owner of 100 shares receives an additional five shares, then the pool of stock increases by five percent, while the total equity value of the outstanding stock remains the same.

Stock Splits

Stock splits can be defined as an action taken by a publicly traded company to increase their number of outstanding shares without increasing the company's market capitalization. Companies split their stocks for a number of reasons. Typically, companies split their stock when the price of the stock has risen to the point of becoming difficult to trade in round lots of 100 shares.

For example, if a company initially offers 1,000,000 shares of stock at $10 per share, and the stock increases to $100 per share, the company may opt for splitting the stock to make it available to smaller investors. A two for one split on a $100 stock would double the number of outstanding shares but leave its capitalization unchanged with a $50 stock price.

The capitalization of the company would have increased from $10 million to $100 million on the 1 million original shares sold. After a two for one stock split, the outstanding shares would have increased to 2 million shares at $50 per share, but the company's market cap would continue to be $100 million.

Stock Split Ratios

The most common ratios that companies use for stock splits are two for one, three for one and three for two; nevertheless, companies can use any ratio the wish when spitting their stock. In the case of a stock that has seen a large increase, stock splits of ten to one or twenty to one are not uncommon.

Microsoft is an example of a large company that has split its stock numerous times, with nine stock splits since 1987. Microsoft has had two-for-one stock splits seven times and three-for-two stock splits two times. Microsoft's most recent stock split occurred in 2003, when the company had a two for one stock split.

If an investor had bought 1,000 shares of Microsoft in 1987 before any stock splits, they would have a total of 288,000 shares of Microsoft stock today after adjusting for the nine stock splits. An investment of $10,000 in Microsoft stock made in 2008 would have a total return of more than 180 percent and a marked to market value of over $28,000 today.

Reverse Stock Splits

While a company's stock that has seen substantial appreciation would be an ideal candidate for a stock split, a company that has seen their stock depreciate substantially would take an opposite strategy to adjust their stock price known as a reverse stock split.

As the name implies, a reverse stock split involves revaluing shares on a ratio such as one for two or one for ten. If a company's stock has declined to $0.25 per share, the company may want to have a reverse stock split of one for ten, in which case the ten shares at $0.25 per share would become one share at $2.50.

In the above example, a holder of 10,000 shares would be left with a revalued position of 1,000 shares at 10 times the price; however, their equity position would not change. Reverse stock splits take place to typically gain more respectability for a company after their stock has seen a prolonged decline, or to avoid the stock being delisted from an exchange, which generally have a minimum share price for stocks to trade at.

CHAPTER 4: COMMODITY MARKET FUNDAMENTALS

Performing fundamental analysis for commodities typically involves looking at the relative supply and demand status of the commodity being traded, including the fundamental of any industries and/or manufactured products that the commodity is used in.

It can also involve performing a detailed market overview, including production sources, industrial uses, legal, regulatory and weather environments, the stability of established price fixing programs like cartels, and consumer confidence in and demand for the commodity or its downstream products.

Some fundamental commodity analysts will review the prospects for one commodity relative to another to assess whether or not the commodity seems cheap or expensive. In addition to being used to establish outright positions, this type of analysis can be used to establish spread positions where the expensive commodity is sold while the cheaper commodity is purchased.

The following sections will introduce each form of analysis, although a very detailed treatment of these important topics lies beyond the scope of this book and is definitely a worthwhile topic for further reading.

Using Fundamental Analysis to Trade Commodities

Fundamental analysis of a commodity generally involves going over the commodity's supply and demand profile. Some analysts may also review relevant data for related or competing commodities, as well as information for the economy as a whole, including economic indicators, government fiscal policies, social and political factors, natural disasters, and interest and inflation rates.

Even the weather reports are relevant fundamental information for some commodities, such as those produced by agricultural concerns since adverse weather conditions can affect supply.

Fundamental analysis uses such information as a way of forecasting price trends. While this technique commonly appeals to those traders with an education in economics, business, accounting or corporate finance, just about anyone can learn to determine what fundamental factors move the commodity markets.

This detailed form of analysis allows commodity traders to get a sense of how one commodity is valued relative to another similar commodity in its sector and to the commodity market as a whole. They can then take that into account given the future prospects for supply and demand in order to develop a view on the commodity's future price.

The rest of this section will describe the basics of fundamental analysis and how to use its techniques to trade commodities.

Commodity Fundamental Analysis Introduced

In the world of commodities trading, fundamental analysis for commodities involves reviewing the factors directly impacting commodity prices on a regular basis. The fundamentals affecting commodity prices depend on things like:

- The nature of the commodity,
- The supply and demand of the commodity in question,
- Weather impacting major agricultural areas,
- The political stability of the region where the commodity is mined, produced or grown, and
- Other macroeconomic factors.

Commodities make up a large group of different types of resources. Some commodities require mining for example like gold, iron, silver, etc. Others are grown such as grains, beans, fruits and spices, while still others come from drilling like crude oil and natural gas.

Furthermore, some commodities are elaborated or manufactured from other commodities. These might include products like unleaded gasoline, soybean oil, steel and plastics, to name just a few. Other commodities are raised such as cattle and hogs.

Each different type of commodity can be affected by a different set of factors or fundamentals, and fundamental traders typically analyze these different factors to help them determine the most likely overall future direction in commodity prices.

Although a detailed treatment of fundamental analysis is beyond the scope of this introductory book, some of the principal factors in the fundamental analysis for commodities will be covered at a basic level in the following sections.

Supply and Demand

The underlying reason for all commodities price movements involves the ubiquitous forces of supply and demand. This particular factor in the fundamental analysis for commodities has to do with the production and consumption respectively of a given commodity.

Take oil for example. If the world's production of oil begins to lag because of dwindling reserves in Saudi Arabia for example, or if the war in the Middle East expanded, this would invariably increase the price of oil. In turn, this would thereby increase the prices of a myriad of other products elaborated with oil because of rising transportation costs due to higher oil prices.

By the same token, if an electric car was suddenly popularized and a quarter of all cars sold were electric, this would also impact the price of oil. Presumably, gasoline consumption would be drastically cut as a result, and so crude oil prices would plummet.

Weather

In general, all agricultural commodities are subject to weather conditions. If an unseasonable freeze hits a crop, this will invariably impact the commodity price, as will an unseasonable heat wave or a flood.

Basically, such extreme weather conditions will tend to increase prices of agricultural commodities, while ideal conditions and a favorable crop and harvest will adversely impact the price due to raised expectations of an increased supply.

Political Factors

A number of political factors potentially impact commodities prices such as elections, political stability of a commodity-producing country, as well as wars and domestic political problems.

Strikes and labor disputes can also directly affect the levels of supply, especially in a commodity such as copper or coal, while a coup d'état or change in political regime could disrupt entire commodity-producing nations.

Economic Factors

The value of money and interest rates also has considerable influence on commodity prices. If interest rates increase, the storage, maintenance and production costs for many commodities rises, thereby directly affecting prices.

Conversely, with lower interest rates, the cost of production decreases and in effect makes commodities prices lower. Inflationary and deflationary cycles, as well as the economic health of individual commodity producer and consumer nations, often have a strong influence on what commodity prices will be.

How Currencies can Affect Commodity Prices

Since market prices represent the equilibrium balance point between supply and demand in the commodity expressed in a particular national fiat currency, the resulting price also reflects the commodity's value relative to that of the currency in which it is quoted.

Another currency-related factor is that some industrial users of commodities import them from other countries. This means they may have considerable exchange rate risks that can affect their choices of what commodity to use in producing goods for sale.

Accordingly, another fundamental factor is the relative valuation prospects of the national currency that the commodity is traded in. As a result, fundamental data relevant to that quotation currency can also be reviewed by an analyst when attempting to predict directional movements for the commodity's price.

Why Use Fundamental Analysis?

Basically, fundamental analysis for commodities trading can be quite beneficial for novice and seasoned traders alike. It also really helps newer traders get a deeper understanding of the factors that move the markets they are considering trading.

In addition, many traders use fundamental analysis to assess the prospects for long term price movements while using technical analysis to time market entry and exit points.

Used together, fundamental and technical analysis can help a trader get a more complete picture about a commodity's future prospects, and so it is well worth investing time in learning how to analyze fundamental information relevant to commodities if you want to trade them successfully.

Fundamental Data for Commodities

As noted in the previous section, fundamental analysis of a commodity generally involves going over the commodity's production supply and commercial use demand profile in detail. Production analysis for soft commodities tends to look at the conditions faced by farmers, while fundamental analysts tend to look at what conditions miners are experiencing for hard commodities.

Fundamental traders also often pay particular attention to factors that might result in industrial users or consumers preferring one commodity over another in an effort to identify commodity spread trades by finding commodities that are over or under priced relative to others.

Furthermore, the release dates and results for key information about the U.S. economy, inflation and interest rates, which will be covered in detail in Chapter 5, are important for fundamental commodity traders. Such releases can involve considerable market volatility if the actual release differs significantly from the market's consensus expectation. Even the weather that might affect a particular commodity will often be closely monitored by commodity analysts and traders.

Key Economic Data

The release dates of key economic numbers that pertain to the economy as a whole where commodities are traded are widely tabulated in economic calendars. The list below includes most of the key economic data releases that reporting agencies within the various countries provide to the market on a regular basis as indicated.

- **Employment Data** – Released monthly
- **Gross Domestic Product (GDP)** – Released quarterly
- **Trade Balance** – Released monthly
- **Retail Sales** – Released monthly
- **Industrial Production** – Released monthly
- **Consumer Price Index (CPI)** – Released monthly
- **Producer Price Index (PPI)** – Released monthly.

Note that the precise times when such releases occur can result in considerable market volatility if the actual number released differs significantly from what the market is expecting as market-makers scramble to discount the new information into the price.

Other Types of Fundamental Information

In addition to the aforementioned economic data, some of the other important fundamental information commonly used by traders and economists in performing fundamental analysis for commodities might include the following:

- Interest and inflation rate levels
- Supply and demand effects relevant to a particular commodity
- Political influences
- Geopolitical events
- Commodity prices
- Survey results
- The Commitment of Traders or COT positioning reports.

While the economic indicators will be covered in detail for the U.S. economy in Chapter 5, several of these additional types of fundamental information will be discussed in the following sections of this chapter.

Weather and Commodities Prices

As mentioned briefly in previous sections, weather and weather related issues can directly influence prices of a wide variety of commodities. The first and most obvious weather risk involves agriculture. Weather has been a key element in the growing of crops since agriculture began thousands of years ago.

The rest of this section gives an overview of how weather can affect commodities prices.

Weather and Agricultural Commodities

Crops need several basic things to be successful, and one of them involves good weather. Having good weather will increase the yield a farmer will have at harvest and also increases the overall supply of the agro-commodity. This scenario repeated by thousands of farmers results in a bumper crop in that agro-commodity, making the price of the agro-commodity plummet.

On the other hand, an unseasonable rainy season or a prolonged winter storm for example could destroy a large portion of the agro-commodity crop reducing supplies and consequently driving the price higher.

Weather also plays a key role in the transporting of commodities and the ability of producers to get their products to market. An important and often overlooked way that the weather can directly influence commodity prices involves transportation costs, because prices rise when transportation costs rise.

Oil, Transportation and Weather-Related Consumption

Transportation of goods and commodities depends directly on the price of oil to fix shipping costs. While railways still account for a sizeable portion of shipping, trucks and ships which use diesel and gasoline make up a large percentage of the shipping industry. The price of oil also impacts many by-products of the petroleum industry such as plastics and petrochemicals for example.

Inclement winter weather drives demand for heating oil up as well as natural gas, coal and other fuels used for heating homes and buildings. A prolonged cold spell or heavy snowfall directly impacts consumption of many commodities and hence affects the supply, driving prices higher.

Other Weather Considerations

When weather in China destroys the wheat crop due to an early monsoon season, U.S. wheat prices can skyrocket. Furthermore, adverse weather in South America can positively affect the price of coffee, and prolonged droughts can affect the price of most affected agricultural commodities, usually causing prices to rise due to their presumed future scarcity.

When Hurricane Katrina hit the U.S. Gulf Coast, many oil refineries were temporarily knocked out of commission affecting gasoline prices worldwide. The price of gasoline in the United States rose considerably until supplies were later secured from other sources, bringing prices back down.

Weather affects us all directly, and in many cases will affect the food you put on your table, the gas that runs your car and the price you pay for a cup of coffee. Basically, weather can affect entire economies and can hinder or prosper a society like no other single factor.

Many professional commodities traders study weather patterns to get an edge on their trading. Weather has become such a decisive factor in the world commodities market that an industry for trading weather futures has emerged. Commodities traders and other speculators can now trade and hedge the weather risk of their positions with futures contracts on the weather in the commodity producing region.

Macroeconomic and Political Commodity Price Factors

Outside of the effects that weather and natural disasters have on commodities prices, macroeconomics and political reasons for commodities prices tend to be the second main cause for price movements in the commodities markets. History offers many instances of how political and macroeconomic events have directly influenced the prices of commodities.

In fact, just open up a newspaper to see the latest news from the Middle East or Venezuela to get an idea about how the price of a barrel of oil might be changing based on a political event. You can also review current Consumer Price Index readings that gauge inflation to see how they impact the price of gold.

The rest of this section discusses how macroeconomics and political events can influence commodities prices.

Political Events

Since commodities typically consist of food, raw materials or manufactured products, a great deal of human energy must be expended in the production, distribution and storage of commodities. Therefore, if political uncertainty looms in a region that either produces or manufactures a commodity, disruption in its supply may ensue, thereby creating a shortage.

For example, unrest in the Middle East offers the most immediate example of how political events can directly influence commodities prices. During both times that the United States went to war with Iraq, initially in 1990 and again in 2003, the prices of crude oil, gasoline and heating oil all rose. When supply sources were reestablished or new sources found, the commodities prices then declined.

Another way that politics can directly affect commodities prices is during election periods. Consider the example of a commodity-producing country with a large industrial base centered on a particular commodity such as copper. If elections are held in that country, the risk of nationalization of that commodity can affect not only the price of copper, but the share prices of the foreign corporations that previously had an interest in the industry in that country.

Such was the case in Chile in 1970 with the election of Salvador Allende. As a left-wing socialist, Allende nationalized the copper industry and subsequently died in a coup d'état in 1973. Other notable nationalizations have involved the oil reserves in Mexico in the 1930s and also those in Venezuela in the 1970s.

Macroeconomic Reasons for Commodity Price Shifts

Commodity prices have fallen under significant pressure since the 1980s when many third-world producers of a large number of different commodities, as well as the nations of Eastern Europe and the Russian Republic, began exporting their goods.

While a healthy world demand was ready to absorb the surplus, commodity prices declined nevertheless. In general, they have shown weakness ever since, with some notable exceptions like gold and oil.

Macroeconomic news affects commodities prices in a variety of ways. Some elements affect all commodities uniformly such as interest rates, while other factors that can directly influence commodity prices include:

- Where the commodities-producing country is in its

business cycle
- A country's money supply
- Whether the overall price situation is inflationary or deflationary
- Gross Domestic and National Product
- Currency exchange rates
- The general level of economic activity.

Macroeconomics and politics can therefore be acknowledged as principal factors in the market's pricing of commodities since they relate directly to the global market forces of supply and demand. As a result, most professional commodity traders keep a watchful eye on political events and economic numbers to obtain an edge in their trading.

Commodity Spread Trading

One important fundamental factor that keeps the prices of related commodities in line with each other is known as commodity spread trading. Commodities spread trading can be defined as trading the price differential between two or more commodities futures contracts.

Spread trading requires somewhat greater sophistication than normal futures trading, largely because knowledge of each commodity is imperative if the spread trader expects to be profitable. Spreads commonly traded with commodities futures also often involve different products of the same basic commodity.

For example, some professional traders speculate on spreads such as crude oil against gasoline, which is commonly known as the "Crack Spread", while other spread traders might prefer speculating on spreads involving agricultural products like the soybean complex.

The rest of this section discusses some of the fundamental factors involved in commodity spread trading.

Why Commodities of Different Months Trade at Different Prices

Commodities generally have carrying costs, in other words, the price for a near-term commodities contract will generally cost less than one that is further out in time because of the costs involved in storing the commodity over time.

For example, a near term futures contract on gold will most likely be less expensive than a contract that is for delivery at a later time. A standard gold contract is usually for 100 ounces of almost-pure gold, and a storage premium will typically be paid for the gold futures contract that has a delivery date six months from the time the contract is purchased. This reflects the carrying and storage costs for the 100 ounces of gold over that period.

Furthermore, if interest rates rise, the carrying cost on the far-term contract will reflect the rise the spread between the near and far-term contracts widening. This example illustrates how a futures contract spread can widen because of an interest rate change that affects the cost of carrying a position.

Other Factors That Influence Commodities Spreads

Each commodity has its own reasons to merit a spread. In agricultural commodities, spreads can widen or narrow depending on inclement weather, as well as on other factors that might affect supply and demand for the commodity.

Also, seasonal factors play a major role in how agricultural commodities contracts can be spread profitably. Corn contracts, for example, typically rise when approaching the December delivery date, while the July contracts usually fall as they approach delivery.

The December contract rises because of an increase in demand for corn during the winter months, while the July contract falls, because of a lower demand for corn during the summer months.

The Soybean Complex

The pricing of some spreads in the commodities market reflect differences in supply and demand of products derived from a basic commodity. Soybeans provide one such example, and soybean contracts can be spread against products that use soybeans for their production such as soybean meal and soybean oil.

Commonly known as the "Crush Spread", this spread involves a trading speculating that the price of soybean oil and meal will change relative to that of the basic soybean product. They would enter this spread by buying or selling the soybean contracts and then simultaneously selling or buying soybean oil and soybean meal contracts against the soybean contracts.

The ratio classically used in this crush spread derives from the fact that one bushel of crushed soybeans will generally produce 11 pounds of soybean oil and 44 pounds of soybean meal. In addition to being traded by speculators, this spread can be used by soybean processors to hedge their production of oil and meal.

Commodity spread trading will generally be performed by more experienced traders since it requires a deeper understanding of the market to be profitable. Nevertheless, margins for spreads are typically lower than for outright futures contract trades, as are the resulting risks and returns.

Using Commodity Fundamentals in Practice

When performing a fundamental analysis on a particular commodity, traders will look at as many fundamental factors as possible for producers and users operating within the relevant economy or economies if cross-border trade is common for that particular commodity. Analysts will take all this data into account, as well as the strength of the currency the commodity is denominated in, when making their price recommendations and trading decisions.

Fundamental traders do this in order to obtain a broad sense of what a particular commodity market's internal, economic and political operating climate is, as well as to determine what growth opportunities exist with respect to demand for the commodity and whether it is suitably valued relative to its competitors.

Basically, if the fundamental data looks better for the commodity relative to others it competes with, then that would tend to imply a rising forecast for its price relative to its competitors. On the other hand, if the commodity's data comes across as weaker relative to others it competes with, then a falling forecast would tend to ensue for its market price relative to its competition.

The commodity's price might still rise in a rising market, especially if inflation is high and the currency in which it is denominated is weak, but probably not as much as other commodities that offer better value. A neutral forecast would tend to result when prospects are roughly the same on balance for commodity relative to others it competes with given their pricing, as long as the underlying market is stable.

Once having made such a forecast, the fundamental commodity trader would then look for opportunities to position themselves in the market to take advantage of the forecast movements in the commodity's price. Over time, they would update this analysis as relevant news events, weather reports and economic data releases occur, and they would adjust their trading position in the commodity accordingly.

Commodity Valuation Factors

As mentioned in the previous sections, the worth of a commodity is generally expressed in terms of the currency it is quoted in. Furthermore, this market price responds sensitively to long-term economic and interest rate cycles, as well as to shifts in policies, production efficiency and consumer demand.

Although economic theorists might postulate that commodity market price fluctuations form an essentially random walk through time, and some even use this hypothetical assumption when developing theoretical commodity option pricing models, for example, almost any cursory review of a chart of a commodity price plotted over time will probably convince you otherwise.

Basically, commodity prices often show remarkable tendencies to trend in a particular direction over time, often as a response to underlying fundamental factors.

The Impact of Inflation on Commodity Prices

Local inflation rates can also result in persistent underlying market trends when a commodity is expressed in the affected currency, and this can affect individual commodity valuations since commodity prices tend to rise overall along with inflation.

This has given certain commodities, like the precious metals for example, the reputation of being an inflation hedge for long term investors.

Basically, if the supply and demand factors for a commodity remain fairly consistent, then its price tends to rise along with that of other commodities due to inflation.

Technical Factors

The repeatability of the aggregate behavior of large groups of humans reviewing a similar set of fundamental information about a market and experiencing similar psychological effects from price action often reflects itself in the formation of recognizable technical price patterns. These in turn set up reliable outcomes that commodity traders can observe and exploit.

While outside the scope of this book, such phenomena are detailed in Volume 2 of this series that focuses on applying technical analysis methods to the financial markets.

Many commodity traders use such so-called price chart patterns to forecast future commodity price movements in virtually any time frame they occur in. Their presence can also substantially move a market to fulfill their objectives as participants see the patterns forming or breaking out and trade accordingly.

CHAPTER 5: U.S. ECONOMIC INDICATORS EXPLAINED

The first thing to understand about economic indicators is that they are specific to each major economy. The largest and perhaps most important economy is that of the United States, so that will be used an example and reference point in this book to get you started on understanding economic indicators in general.

Furthermore, when it comes to being successful as a financial markets trader, time is of the essence when making trading decisions based on economic releases. As a result, you will probably need to keep in mind all of the relevant and important market-moving economic indicators and have an economic calendar kept close to hand that lays out their release dates and times.

Professional traders typically remain glued to their news wire screens that report releases as soon as they come out, and they always make sure to research what the market is expecting prior to a big data release. Due to the notable volatility that can accompany the release of some of these indicators, many more conservative traders prefer to square or substantially reduce their positions ahead of the time the results are announced to the public.

Any significant deviation in the current results or a notable revision to the previously-announced results for a major data release will tend to move the market either up or down depending on its implications. Many fundamental traders will memorize the likely impact of a deviation from expectations on the market, or they will at least look it up or consult with their in-house economist prior to the announcement.

The following sections of this chapter are intended to be used as reference material for fundamental analysts interested in operating in markets potentially affected by U.S. economic indicators, with the primary focus being on the forex market since the relative valuation of the U.S. Dollar versus other currencies can be notably affected by shifts and trends in these indicators.

The reader will note that the section devoted to each major U.S. economic indicator includes: its name, its source, what it measures, what effect it has on the U.S. Dollar, how often it is released, and why traders consider it important. Finally, since this information can change over time, it is important to take this reference section as a general guide to these indicators, but do be sure to review the specifics of each indicator with the releasing source before trading based on this information.

The Capacity Utilization Rate

The Capacity Utilization Rate is sometimes also known as the Operating Rate and is released by The Federal Reserve Board's Statistical Releases Department.

What it Measures

In macroeconomics, the Capacity Utilization Rate is the economy's total percentage of factories, equipment and mines that are currently producing. In other words, Capacity Utilization measures the percentage of an industry, or country's capacity for production which is actually used over a particular time period.

For example, if a company produces 50 units of a product in a day with the possibility of producing 50 more units without their production costs rising, then the company is running at a 50% Capacity Utilization Rate.

What Effect it Has

If the U.S. Capacity Utilization Rate comes out higher-than-expected, that usually appreciates the U.S. currency, while a lower-than-expected number will prompt the U.S. Dollar's decline.

For other countries than the United States, a rising Capacity Utilization Rate will indicate strength in a national economy and will be favorable to the currency of that country when the actual rate of Capacity Utilization is higher than that forecast by economists. Conversely, a decline in the rate would indicate that the economy of that nation was weakening and would tend to depreciate the currency.

How often it is Released

The Capacity Utilization Rate is released monthly and is periodically revised along with the related Industrial Production number. In the United States, both of these economic data releases usually come out 16 days after the month ends and come directly from the Federal Reserve.

Why it is Important

In essence, Capacity Utilization acts as a leading indicator of consumer inflation since industries will tend to incur higher production costs as industry approaches full capacity, thereby passing on higher costs to consumers.

Furthermore, an expanding economy will demonstrate a rising percentage of Capacity Utilization, while a decreasing Capacity Utilization Rate will signal a contracting economy. Also, Capacity Utilization tends to signal a lower potential for growth when an economy is running near full capacity. Weather and other factors can directly influence Industrial Production which is then in turn reflected in the Capacity Utilization Rate.

The Consumer Confidence Index

The Conference Board's Consumer Confidence Index or simply the Consumer Confidence Index is related in terms of what it measures to The University of Michigan Consumer Sentiment Index.

The Consumer Confidence Index is released by The Conference Board, a non-profit independent business group dedicated to economic research which has calculated the Index since 1967.

What it Measures

The CB's Consumer Confidence Index measures the level of optimism (or lack of it) of the average U.S. consumer about their financial health which is expressed through their spending and savings activities. The index is calculated by surveying 5,000 U.S. households asking each household their opinions in five key areas:

1. Current business conditions

2. Business conditions for the next six months
3. Current employment conditions
4. Employment conditions for the next six months
5. Total family income for the next six months

Once the results of the surveys are collected, the questions with positive results are divided by the sum of the positive and negative answers. The result is then compared to the benchmark of 1985, which represents the mid-level of the business cycle and is given a value of 100, to create a composite index.

What Effect it Has

If the Consumer Confidence Index comes out higher-than-expected, that usually appreciates the U.S. Dollar. On the other hand, a lower-than-expected Consumer Confidence number will prompt the Dollar's decline.

The Conference Board's Consumer Confidence Index is one of the most widely watched of all fundamental indicators, and its revisions can also prompt significant market activity. It tends to act as a leading indicator and its movements can influence equity prices, currency exchange rates and interest-rate policy for the Federal Reserve.

How often it is Released

Results of the Conference Board's Consumer Confidence Survey are released the last Tuesday of each month at 10 AM EST.

Why it is Important

In general, Consumer Confidence expresses the optimism of the average U.S. consumer with an increase in consumer confidence indicating economic growth simply because consumers are spending money and therefore stimulating the economy. A decrease in consumer confidence would imply that consumers are spending less, hence indicating a decrease in economic growth. Many businesses as well as banks, manufacturers and the government watch the Consumer Confidence Index to base decisions on production, lending activity, taxes and interest rates.

Furthermore, the Consumer Confidence Index shows the public's perception about the ability to obtain and secure jobs and therefore on how they will spend their income. If the index is in an overall downtrend, consumers will hold back on making large purchases which impacts manufacturers of big-ticket items such as automobiles. Banks are also impacted by a reduction in lending activity and mortgage applications while the government might need to reduce interest rates or offer a tax rebate to stimulate the economy.

If Consumer Confidence is rising, on the other hand, manufacturers can hire more people and increase production while growing demand for credit will increase banking profits, and the government can also expect an increase in tax revenues. A rising index will generally affect currency prices favorably while a declining index will have an inverse effect.

Another widely-watched monthly economic release related to consumer confidence is The University of Michigan Consumer Sentiment Index. This report is based on a telephone survey that gathers information about how people feel about the overall economy.

The Consumer Price Index or CPI

The Consumer Price Index or CPI is also sometimes known as the Headline Inflation rate. It is also released along with the Core CPI number that excludes Food and Energy sectors that tend to be volatile. The CPI is released by the U.S. Bureau of Labor Statistics.

What it Measures

The Consumer Price Index or CPI is sometimes also called "headline inflation" and consists of a weighted average that measures the change in prices of a fixed basket of consumer goods and services that are weighted in order of importance. Goods include such items as: food, housing, transportation, medical care, recreation, education and apparel.

Core CPI is the weighted average of price changes for goods and services, with food and energy prices excluded. Food and energy products account for a quarter of the CPI which can give an unreliable picture of the overall inflationary trend because of the volatility in these commodities.

As a result, the Federal Reserve and top economists usually prefer using Core CPI to gauge actual levels of inflation in the economy to adjust interest rates accordingly. Currency traders also use Core CPI since it is a more precise and less volatile gauge of inflation.

What Effect it Has

If the U.S. Consumer Price Index or CPI or Core CPI number comes out higher-than-expected, that usually appreciates the U.S. Dollar. On the other hand, a lower-than-expected number will tend to prompt the Dollar's decline.

CPI, and in particular Core CPI, is one of the most widely-watched of all fundamental indicators, and its revisions can also result in significant market activity. CPI movements can influence equity prices and currency exchange rates due to its implications for interest-rate policy set by the Federal Reserve.

How often it is Released

The Bureau of Labor Statistics releases the Consumer Price Index monthly, typically between the 13th and 19th of the month. The monthly report is for the preceding month.

Why it is Important

Changes in the prices of consumer goods are perhaps the most direct measure of inflationary forces in the economy. A rising CPI will indicate that the economy is in an inflationary cycle and the value of money is declining. In order to contain inflation, the Federal Reserve may respond by raising interest rates and this in turn will affect all other areas of the U.S. economy. A falling CPI, on the other hand, indicates a deflationary environment which may prompt the Fed to reduce rates.

In general, the level of inflation in the economy affects all consumers. Also, the Federal Reserve relies partly on this key CPI data to formulate monetary policy since the central bank has an inflation containment mandate and so will need to raise rates to contain inflation or lower interest rates in the face of deflation. Each of these adjustments will in turn affect prices, economic activity and the valuation of the country's currency.

The Fed's Beige Book

The Fed's Beige Book is formally known as *The Summary of Commentary on Current Economic Conditions* and is also called: *Current Economic Conditions*. It is a composite written report that is released by The U.S. Federal Reserve Bank.

What it Measures:

A summary of 12 Federal Reserve district reports is commonly-known as the Fed's Beige Book, or more formally as *The Summary of Commentary on Current Economic Conditions*. This influential Book is prepared by one of the Federal Reserve Banks given the task on a rotating basis.

Basically, the twelve regional Reserve Banks of the Federal Reserve System compile "anecdotal" information of economic conditions in each of the twelve Federal Reserve regions. Each Reserve bank obtains information for the Beige Book through reports from other major banks and their branch directors as well as from interviews with economists, market experts and key business contacts and summarizes the information by District and sector.

What Effect it Has

The Fed's Beige Book report typically affects the market by expressing the general tone of the Federal Reserve towards interest rates and prevailing economic conditions.

If the Book's overall tone is interpreted by the market as more hawkish-than-expected, thereby indicating a tendency for the Fed to raise interest rates, this usually has a positive effect on the U.S. Dollar relative to other currencies.

How often it is Released

The Fed's Beige Book is released eight times a year, two Wednesdays before the meeting of the FOMC in that given month. Beige Books are therefore released in January, March, April, June, July, September, October and December.

Why it is Important

The Fed's Beige Book represents the assessment of the Federal Reserve of the economic conditions of each of its 12 districts. The economic factors it examines on a local level directly impacts the Federal Reserve's decisions on interest rates which is extremely important to the economic prospects of the nation.

In essence, this publicly-available book is relied upon by the Federal Open Market Committee or FOMC to make decisions on monetary policy, although the FOMC also uses two other books that are not released to the public. These are the Fed's Blue and Green Books that are considered even more influential on the Fed's interest rate decisions.

The Gross Domestic Product or GDP

The Gross Domestic Product or GDP is released by the Bureau of Economic Analysis of the U.S. Department of Commerce.

What it Measures

The Gross Domestic Product or GDP is the net worth of the sum of all that is produced in a country along with services, investments, public expenditures, government outlays, and the balance of trade measured annually.

In essence, the GDP measures the national standard of living as well as the overall economic health in the country and so holds an important place among the fundamental indicators of any country.

What Effect it Has

If the U.S. Gross Domestic Product number comes out higher-than-expected, that usually appreciates the U.S. Dollar. On the other hand, a lower-than-expected number will prompt the Dollar's decline. GDP is one of the most widely watched of all fundamental indicators, and its revisions can also prompt significant market activity.

GDP movements can influence equity prices, currency exchange rates and interest-rate policy for the Federal Reserve.

How often it is Released

Gross Domestic Product or GDP is a quarterly report released with an annualized change that consists of the change for the quarter times four. The advance GDP release comes out four weeks after the end of the quarter, while the final release comes out three months after the end of the quarter.

Why it is Important

The GDP has an enormous effect on the economy, with rising GDP manifesting as businesses hire and expand to meet rising demand for products, goods are exported and the business cycle shows a growing economy. While a declining GDP signals a slowdown of the economy when demand for products wane and the business cycle moves toward recession.

Furthermore, the indicator is the most important indicator in determining if the economy is healthy and growing or slipping into recession. Economists and traders rely on this indicator which typically indicates a healthy economy when growing at a 3% to 3.5% rate. At these moderate levels, the indicator will not signal an excess of inflation.

Basically, GDP is the broadest indicator for gauging the health of a country's economy and so is closely-watched by the Federal Reserve in the United States to determine the strength of the economy in order to adjust interest rates and monetary policy.

Major Housing Market Indicators

The major U.S. housing market-related indicators and their sources include:

- The FHFA House Price Index or HPI is released by the Federal Housing Finance Agency.

- The S&P/CS Composite-20 House Price Index is released by Standard and Poor's.

- Building Permits, Housing Starts and New Home Sales are released by the Census Bureau.

- Pending Home Sales and Existing Home Sales are released by the National Association of Realtors.

What They Measure

All of these related indicators measure some aspect of the housing market as follows:

- *FHFA House Price Index* – Measures the change in the purchase price of homes with mortgages backed by the Federal National Mortgage Association or Fannie Mae and the Federal Mortgage Acceptance Corporation or Freddie Mac.

- *S&P/CS Composite-20 HPI* – Measures the change in the selling price of single-family homes in 20 metropolitan areas.

- *Building Permits* - the amount of new residential building permits issued in the previous month.

- *Housing Starts* - the annualized number of new residential buildings that started construction the previous month.

- *New Home Sales* - The annualized number of new single-family homes that sold during the previous month.

- *Pending Home Sales* – Measures the change in the number of homes contracted to be sold but still waiting for the closing transaction, excluding new construction.

- *Existing Home Sales* – The annualized number of residential buildings that were sold the previous month, excluding new construction.

What Effect They Have

If the actual housing market number comes out greater than a consensus of economists forecast, then that will tend to raise the value of the currency, and vice versa.

How often they are Released

- *FHFA House Price Index or HPI*– released monthly, typically 55 days after the end of the month reviewed.

- *S&P/CS Composite-20 HPI* – released monthly, typically 60 days after the end of the month reviewed.

- *Building Permits* – released monthly, typically 17 days after the end of the month reviewed.

- *Housing Starts* - released monthly, typically 17 days after the end of the month reviewed.

- *New Home Sales* – released monthly, typically 25 days after the end of the month reviewed.

- *Pending Home Sales* – released monthly, typically 35 days after the end of the month reviewed.

- *Existing Home Sales* – released monthly, typically 24 days after the end of the month reviewed.

Why They are Important

The housing market is a major indicator of the nation's overall economic health and has a domino effect on the rest of the economy. More building means more construction workers are employed which adds money to the economy in the form of consumer spending and creates more jobs.

In addition, construction requires material that also adds to the flow of money into the economy and home sales require mortgages which stimulate the banking sector. Many more aspects of the economy are affected by the housing market and directly affect the overall economic health of the nation.

Basically, housing and building construction are one of the basic activities in an expanding economy. When housing and building starts begin to show weakness, it is a leading indication that the rest of the economy will soon follow suit. This makes the housing indicators extremely important to anyone involved in banking and investment, as well as to the Federal Reserve which uses these indicators, among others, to determine how they deal with interest rate and monetary policy.

Industrial Production

Industrial Production or IP is also known as Factory Output and is released by The Federal Reserve Bank.

What it Measures

Industrial Production is an inflation-adjusted index that measures the total real output of the manufacturing, mining and electric and gas utilities which account for the major part of variation in national output throughout the business cycle.

The index is expressed as a percentage real output of the base year, which is currently 2002.

What Effect it Has

If the Industrial Production number comes out higher-than-expected, that usually appreciates the U.S. Dollar, while a lower-than-expected number will prompt the Dollar's decline.

How often it is Released

The data is released monthly, typically 16 days after the end of the month reviewed.

Why it is Important

Industrial Production is a leading economic indicator that, despite representing a small percentage of the GDP, is directly-affected by consumer demand and interest rates. It is typically used by banks, the Federal Reserve and economists to predict levels of inflation and economic performance.

Since Industrial Production typically acts as a leading indicator, it shows changes in advance of other economic indicators because it directly reflects consumer demand. With improving Industrial Production, other economic indicators tend to follow suit, although a large increase could be an indication of increasing inflation in the economy.

In addition, Industrial Production acts as an indicator of overall economic health since it is directly-affected by fluctuations in the business cycle that impact corporate profits and employment conditions in the economy. In addition, the Capacity Utilization indicator is directly-related to changes in the Industrial Production indicator, and the two indicators are generally released at the same time each month.

Weekly Initial Jobless Claims

Weekly Initial Jobless Claims is also known as Initial Jobless Claims, Jobless Claims, Initial Claims and Unemployment Claims and the data is released on a weekly basis by the U.S. Department of Labor,

What it Measures

The Jobless Claims report keeps track of how many people have filed for unemployment benefits in the past week. The weekly releases also include a continuing claims report, as well as the initial jobless claims number.

The indicator is useful in gauging the U.S. jobs market and is used by economists, investors and the Federal Reserve to monitor job growth and emerging unemployment trends.

Nevertheless, because of the volatility in the job market reflected by this indicator, it has limited validity and is therefore released with a smoothed-out figure arrived at by taking a four-week moving average in order for analysts to get a better sense of the indicator without the extreme volatility.

What Effect it Has

If the number comes out higher-than-expected, that tends to depreciate the U.S. Dollar because it indicates higher unemployment, and vice versa. Jobless Claims give a timely indication of where the economy is heading, and if considerably different from expectations, they will often affect capital markets significantly upon their release.

How often it is Released

Released weekly, the report comes out every Thursday at 8:30 AM EST.

Why it is Important

As more people file for unemployment benefits, fewer people have jobs reducing consumer spending and causing a further slowdown in the economy. When fewer people file for unemployment benefits, this indicates an expanding economy and increased consumer spending.

Jobless Claims are considered a lagging indicator of the economic situation in the United States because employment tends to be a result of economic trends and so generally lags behind other indicators more initially affected by economic factors. Nevertheless, the number is strongly-associated with consumer spending and with the labor market, so has important economic implications.

Key Employment Data

Non-Farm Payrolls or NFP, also sometimes known as the Non-Farm Employment Change, The Unemployment Rate and the ADP Non-farm Employment Change together make up the key employment data released by the United States.

Non-Farm Payrolls and The Unemployment Rate: are released by the Bureau of Labor Statistics of the U.S. Department of Labor, while the ADP Non-Farm Employment Change is released by Automated Data Processing Systems (ADP).

What They Measures

Non-Farm Payrolls - indicates the amount of jobs from the construction, manufacturing and goods-producing sectors of the economy added or lost over the previous month. The data is for non-farm jobs because the agricultural sector of the economy includes seasonal hiring during the harvest which would distort the data.

Unemployment Rate – indicates the rate of unemployment prevailing in the United States as a percentage of the U.S. work force currently unemployed and seeking employment actively during the preceding month.

ADP Non-farm Employment Change – ADP is a major provider of electronic payrolls for a large number of U.S. corporations. Its employment change report typically appears two days before the U.S. Government employment reports and so is an increasingly-watched indicator since it gives a preview to the key official reports.

What Effect They Have

In general, better-than-expected U.S. employment numbers will raise the value of the U.S. Dollar against other currencies, while disappointing numbers will have the opposite effect. The NFP number is usually the most closely-watched of all U.S. economic data releases and certainly has the greatest significance among the employment numbers.

Because employment generates consumer spending, the Non-Farm Payrolls and other employment indicators are extremely important to the economic well-being of the nation. Increased consumer spending stimulates the economy and in turn creates more jobs to meet greater consumer demand. Nevertheless, it can also prompt a rise in inflationary pressures which the Fed may respond to with higher rates.

How often They are Released

Non-Farm Payrolls and Unemployment Rate – released monthly, typically on the first Friday after the end of the month reviewed.

ADP Non-farm Employment Change - released monthly, typically on the first Wednesday after the end of the month reviewed.

Why They are Important

A reduction of jobs signaling a contracting U.S. economy will directly and adversely affect the currency, equity and debt markets of the United States. Also, a continuing trend toward job reduction will tend to signal a recession.

Conversely, when jobs are expanding, the markets will usually react favorably to that news. Furthermore, a strong increase in jobs could also raise inflationary tendencies, thereby leading the Federal Reserve to tighten interest rates.

Basically, as more people file for unemployment benefits, fewer people have jobs and so this reduces consumer spending and causes a further slowdown in the economy. When fewer people file for unemployment benefits, this indicates an expanding economy and increases the probability of greater consumer spending.

Personal Consumption Expenditure

The Core Personal Consumption Expenditure Price Index or PCE is released by the U.S. Bureau of Economic Analysis. This indicator is also sometimes known as:

- The PCEPI
- Implicit Price Deflator for Personal Consumption Expenditures
- PCE deflator
- PCE price deflator and
- The Chain-type Price Index for Personal Consumption Expenditures or CTPIPCE. This is the name used by the Federal Open Market Committee or FOMC of the Federal Reserve.

What it Measures

The PCE indicator measures the average increase in prices for all U.S. domestic personal consumption. The index has a basis year of 2005 which equals 100 and is derived from the Gross Domestic Product's largest component of personal consumption expenditures that excludes food and energy prices.

The indicator is an inflation measure which has been the Federal Reserve's primary indicator for inflation since it changed from the Consumer Price Index in 2000.

What Effect it Has

If the U.S. Core Personal Consumption Expenditure Price Index number comes out higher-than-expected, the value of the U.S. Dollar usually appreciates. On the other hand, a lower-than-expected number will tend to prompt the Dollar's decline.

While Core CPI is one of the most widely-watched of all fundamental indicators, the Core Personal Consumption Expenditure Price Index can also influence equity prices and currency exchange rates especially due to its implications for interest-rate policy set by the Federal Reserve.

How often it is Released

The PCE is released monthly, typically 30 days after the end of the month reviewed.

Why it is Important

The PCE index is weighted by current period quantities which are variable. This is also known as "chain-type" weighting rather than weighting the index by a fixed basket of goods which is how CPI is calculated.

The index measures current personal consumption in today's prices which it then compares to the current personal consumption of its 2005 base year. By using this method, the index can give a clearer picture of overall inflationary trends in the economy and gives the Federal Reserve a basis upon which to adjust interest rates to manage inflation.

The Producer Price Index

The Producer Price Index or PPI is also known as Finished Goods PPI or Wholesale Prices. It is released by The U.S. Department of Labor.

What it Measures

The Producer Price Index or PPI measures the prices of physical goods at the producer or wholesale level. The weighted index includes all goods manufactured and produced in the U.S. and was called the Wholesale Price Index until 1978.

The PPI consists of price data taken from three levels in the manufacturing cycle:

- *PPI Commodity Index* – also called PPI crude, shows prices for raw materials such as crude oil, coal and scrap steel.

- *PPI Stage of Processing Index* – The SOP as it is also called shows prices for goods which are in the intermediate stage of production which will later be sold to producers to make a finished product.

- *PPI Industry Index* – shows prices for goods at the final stage of manufacture and is the source of the core PPI figure.

PPI uses a fixed basket of goods from 1982, which is given a value of 100, as a benchmark year for measuring increases.

What Effect it Has

If the PPI number is higher than the consensus, this will have a favorable effect on the value of the U.S. Dollar because rising prices at the wholesale level tend to indicate increased demand on the consumer level, as well as a higher risk of interest rate rises.

Conversely, if the number comes out lower-than-expected, it will tend to prompt a decline in the value of the Dollar due to reduced concerns over inflationary pressures.

How often it is Released

The PPI is released monthly, typically 15 days after the end of the month reviewed.

Why it is Important

A leading indicator of inflationary trends in the economy, the PPI is a widely-watched index that is used by the Federal Reserve to gauge inflation at the wholesale level in order to adjust interest rates. As a result, it can have an important impact on the U.S. Dollar.

Furthermore, when wholesale prices increase, these costs are usually passed on to consumers. This therefore increases the likelihood of inflation taking hold in the economy which may prompt the Federal Reserve to raise interest rates.

The Purchasing Manager's Index

The Purchasing Manager's Index or PMI is also sometimes known as the ISM Manufacturing PMI. It is released by The Institute for Supply Management or ISM.

What it Measures

The Purchasing Manager's Index measures the percentage of purchasing managers which reported better business conditions in their industry in the preceding month.

The index is determined by surveying 400 purchasing managers from the manufacturing sector in five areas:
1. Employment,
2. Production,
3. New orders from clients,
4. Speed of deliveries from suppliers and
5. Inventories.

The results from each field are used to determine the percentage of respondents that reported better overall conditions than the previous month. A reading above 50.00 would indicate expansion in the economy, while a number below 50.00 would indicate a contraction in business conditions.

What Effect it Has

A higher-than-expected PMI number is favorable for the U.S. Dollar because it detects inflationary trends and puts pressure on the Federal Reserve to raise interest rates. Conversely, if the number released is lower than expected, it would probably prompt the value of the Dollar to decline.

How often it is Released

The PMI is released monthly, typically on the day after the end of the month reviewed.

Why it is Important

PMI is a leading indicator of health in the U.S. economy because purchasing managers have the most immediate view of economic forces that would affect their business. The indicator gives an accurate view of manufacturing economic activity and is often used to predict the PPI or Producer Price Index.

Also, the indicator is released on the day after the end of the month reviewed which gives a timely view on overall inflationary trends ahead of other indicators that are released later in the month.

Other important related indicators are the Chicago PMI, which surveys purchasing managers from the Chicago area, and the ISM Non-Manufacturing PMI, which surveys purchasing managers for businesses outside of the manufacturing sector.

Retail Sales

Retail Sales is also known as Advance Retail Sales and is released by the U.S. Census Bureau.

What it Measures

Retail Sales measures the total dollar value of sales made at the retail level of the economy. The data is further divided into the following two categories:

- *Consumer Durable Goods* – typically items which last for a minimum of three years.

- *Consumer Non-durable Goods* – items that last for less than three years.

The Retail Sales number is thought to reflect the public's overall purchasing trends, thereby indicating the level of consumer spending.

What effect it has:

Generally, rising Retail Sales is a sign of an economic expansion which is favorable to the U.S. Dollar, so higher-than-expected Retail Sales numbers will tend to boost the Dollar.

A declining trend in the Retail Sales indicator or a lower-than-expected number would tend to indicate the U.S. economy is heading toward recession. This would eventually lead to the Federal Reserve lowering interest rates, which tends to adversely affect the Dollar's value.

How often it is released:

Retail Sales is released on a monthly basis. Releases typically occur around the 14th of the month after the month reviewed at 8:30 am EST.

Why it is Important

Retail Sales figures are an important economic indicator because they give a good general picture of consumer spending. Core Retail Sales, sometimes called "ex-auto" Retail Sales, excludes automobile sales which make up a 20% component of Retail Sales. This figure is more reliable since auto sales tend to be extremely volatile and many fundamental traders prefer to focus on this number instead.

The Retail Sales monthly report also excludes money spent on services, therefore representing only half of total consumption in the economy during the month. Nevertheless, the number is still considered one of the chief fundamental indicators of the economic health of the nation. Retail Sales can therefore have a considerable impact on the currency market if it differs significantly from the market's consensus expectations.

The Trade Balance

The Trade Balance is also known as the Balance of Trade, International Trade or the Trade Deficit. It is released by The U.S. Bureau of Economic Analysis or BEA.

What it Measures

The Trade Balance measures the U.S. Dollar value of all U.S. exports against the Dollar value of all U.S. imports. The indicator also measures trade balances for services such as financial and informational services like computer software.

The United States has run a trade deficit for many years because the value of its imports has exceeded the value of its exports. In part, this shortfall has arisen from the import of foreign oil from the Middle East and consumer goods from China.

The Current Account, which is often cited in a similar context to the Trade Balance especially for countries other than the United States, refers to the difference in the value of exported and imported physical goods, income flows, services and unilateral cash transfers.

What Effect it Has

When the U.S. Trade Balance shows a smaller deficit that was expected that tends to make the value of the Dollar increase. Nevertheless, a Trade Balance deficit that widens more than expected should reduce the value of the Dollar.

Basically, a narrowing trade deficit indicates that foreigners are buying more U.S. goods and therefore need more U.S. Dollars to execute these transactions. This tends to increase demand for Dollars, and hence its value goes up.

How often it is Released

The Trade Balance is released monthly, generally occurring about 40 days after the end of the month reviewed.

Why it is Important

Exports and currencies are directly linked because foreigners must pay for goods with U.S. Dollars. Export demand will also often impact prices for manufacturers and producers of domestic goods and services.

Furthermore, some economists maintain that the Trade Balance should be balanced by foreign investment in U.S. Treasury Securities as foreign investors that export to the U.S. receive payment in U.S. Dollars. Nevertheless, if U.S. interest rates are low, then holding U.S.-backed securities is not as attractive to foreign investors, causing the value of the Dollar to decline.

Imports, on the other hand, must be paid for in local currencies and will increase the value of the currency in the country where that particular product or service is produced.

Basically, the Trade Balance is directly tied in to the demand for a currency and has traditionally been one of the most important numbers that the currency market reacts to.

JAY AND JULIE HAWK

CHAPTER 6: RECOMMENDED FURTHER READING

As endeavors, trading, and the market analysis that drives it, both go back to the age-old beginning of commerce. Fortunately, many successful traders throughout the years have written about their experiences and mistakes so that those newer to trading do not need to repeat them.

For further education on the topic of market analysis as it relates to trading, the reader is first referred to the other book in this market analysis series on technical analysis, as well as to the trading guides to the forex, stock and commodity markets that were also written by these same professional authors.

If you plan on trading via an exchange or online broker, then they should provide websites that their clients can view with details about each asset and contract you are interested in trading. You should review those specifications carefully to make sure you understand the quantities involved and the maturity date. You should also look over any delivery requirements if the contract is not cash settled, which is especially important for commodity traders.

Beyond that, a broader list of recommended literature should probably include books on trading in general, because regardless of what market you are watching, trading or analyzing, traders of every discipline share the same overall experience.

In addition, reading books that go into depth on particular aspects of fundamental analysis will give newer traders deeper insights into this important market analysis discipline that lie beyond the scope of this introductory book.

Classic Books on Trading in General

The first book on trading that comes to mind would have to be "Reminiscences of a Stock Operator" by Edwin Lefevre. Based on the life of Jesse Livermore, this classic book captures the attitudes and mindset of one of the most successful stock traders of the first half of the 20th century. Although the stock market was still young then, the book still gives you a good idea of what goes on in the mind of a remarkably successful trader. Although Livermore traded stocks, many of his experiences and his mindset are very relevant to commodity traders.

Two more recent bestsellers provide a useful perspective on trading for aspiring or seasoned traders alike. "The Market Wizards" and "The New Market Wizards" by Jack Schwager both contain excellent interviews with some of the world's top traders. Together, they give extraordinary insight both into the traders' psychology, as well as into how to profit in specific markets and how such top market players developed their trading systems.

Another fascinating book on trading is "The Complete Turtle Trader" by Michael Covel. The book recounts the famous story of the Turtles — a group of traders that were trained in trend-following by master trader Richard Dennis. He began this experiment as a result of a bet made with colleague William Eckhardt, and it became wildly successful. Nevertheless, some of the subjects of the experiment were not as profitable as others given the same opportunity. The book also lays out the principles and trading rules of the experiment and offers highly-educational reading for anyone serious about trading.

Readings on Technical Analysis

Although many other books are available on the subject of trading, be sure that your reading on the subject includes a more detailed treatment of technical analysis since fundamental analysis alone is rarely sufficient. This set of techniques that use past price action to forecast the future direction of prices has become an essential subject for any trader to get a grasp of, no matter whether they wish to trade in the stock, forex or commodities markets.

For a comprehensive introduction and practical guide to the topic of technical analysis, the reader is referred to these authors' book on the topic that forms the second volume of this market analysis series.

Furthermore, most seasoned technical analysts would agree that an excellent reference book on technical analysis is "Technical Analysis of the Financial Markets: A Comprehensive Guide to Trading Methods and Applications" by John G. Murphy. This book gives a complete overview of all major market and is an invaluable resource for both new and professional traders.

Further Reading on Market Analysis and Trading

In addition to the books by these authors published by Jellyhawk Financial Press, many other fine books on market analysis and trading can be found, and the New York Institute of Finance publishes an especially good collection of books on those topics.

Remember, the more you know about the subject of trading and understand how to analyze the market you have chosen to participate in, the more prepared you will be when you make decisions as a trader.

Basically, when it comes to trading, knowledge really is power, and knowing how to apply that knowledge generally distinguishes successful traders and market analysts from the rest of the pack.

ABOUT THE AUTHORS

Jay and Julie Hawk are a husband and wife team who currently trade forex, stocks, commodities and cryptocurrencies online for their own account and have worked professionally in the financial markets in several different occupations. Together, they have more than 40 years of experience trading in the financial markets and are world-class experts at performing both fundamental and technical analysis to support their trading and risk management activities.

For her part, Julie completed her scientific research degree and started out working as a business systems analyst for a major investment bank where she became qualified as a Series 7 Registered Representative and was thoroughly trained in all major financial products. She also attended the well-known O'Connell and Piper options training course in Chicago. She later worked as a dealer in the trading rooms of several major international banks in New York City, London and San Francisco, eventually working her way up to the vice president level.

In that capacity, Julie was personally involved in educating, providing customized hedging and risk taking strategies, meeting with other corporate executives, and handling large scale transactions for high-profile banking clients including large corporations, fund managers and high net worth individuals. She also traded substantial options portfolios for her employers as a risk manager, including exotic options like binary, barrier, average rate and basket options. She even received a notable award for her creativity, teamwork and profitability in executing unusual and highly profitable derivatives transactions.

During that time, Julie also developed world-class expertise in technical analysis, including Elliott Wave Theory, and was involved in initiating research into automated trading and trading signal systems. She also joined the San Francisco Writers' Guild and regularly wrote trade strategies, educational material, market commentary, market newsletters, reports, articles and press releases. In addition, Julie was interviewed for various financial markets magazines and for news wires such as REUTERS in her professional capacity as a financial markets expert.

In contrast to Julie's highly professional and elite banking role, Jay's professional trading experience was focused more on futures and options exchange floor trading activities, fund management, and fundamental research-based commodity trading and stock investing. After growing up in Chicago and then moving to Mexico City, Jay returned to Chicago to begin working in the futures and options markets on the Chicago Board Options Exchange just a few years after the exchange was founded.

In addition to working his way up to holding a seat and operating as a market maker on several options exchanges in Chicago and San Francisco, Jay also ran a retail stock brokerage desk and managed funds for a number of large institutional investors that he traded profitably on a discretionary basis and that included stock, commodity and forex trades. Jay later took a position on the Chicago Mercantile Exchange where he helped start up and actively traded in a variety of listed futures and options. He eventually moved to the West Coast to start trading on the Pacific Options Exchange, where he focused largely on trading stock options and the underlying stocks.

After both independently retiring from their professional trading careers as relatively wealthy people, Jay and Julie met up, fell love and got married to raise a child together just after the new millennium dawned. They moved to Mexico to semi-retire near the beach and operate an Internet-based business together, but they soon discovered that the financial markets had become far more accessible to retail traders via online brokers and the availability of CFD trading. This incredible opportunity seemed too tempting for these seasoned traders to ignore!

They also observed a demand for educational material to be provided to retail traders via the Internet, and that the quality of existing written content available online was rather poor. That led them to start a new career together as freelance writers specializing in writing about the financial markets using their professional background and expertise. This eventually resulted in them co-founding TheFXperts (located online at www.thefxperts.com) to provide clients with expertly-written market analysis and commentary, informational content about financial markets, trader mentoring and financial consulting.

Jay and Julie are very pleased to present this book on fundamental analysis as the first in a two-part series of books on market analysis that they will be releasing over the coming months to supplement their existing three volume guide to trading the forex, stock and commodity markets. You can visit TheFXperts' website to learn about their future book releases.

JAY AND JULIE HAWK

GLOSSARY

Balance Sheet: A financial statement listing a company's assets, liabilities and allocation of shareholder equity at a particular point in time. The balance sheet allows the public to see what the company owns and how much it owes, as well as the stock ownership of the firm.

Capital Markets: A global marketplace where all financial instruments like commodities, currencies, stocks and bonds are traded.

Closing Price: The final closing amount of money at which an asset has traded at on a given trading day. In markets that trade round the clock, the closing price is determined at a certain hour of the day for the region in which the asset is traded. For example, the CME closes commodity futures trading each weekday at 5:00pm EST and then re-opens for electronic trading at 6pm EST.

Corporation: A legally formed body that is authorized by law to act as a single person regardless of how many people form the body. The corporation is allowed its own rights and duties separate from its members and includes the right of succession.

Cross Rate: The exchange rate between two currencies neither of which is the U.S. Dollar. EUR/JPY and GBP/EUR are two common cross rates.

Currency Futures: Standardized foreign exchange contracts traded on centralized exchanges that involve the purchase of one currency and the sale of another. The delivery date for such transferrable contracts usually falls on particular date, often quarterly, in order to provide greater liquidity, and the futures trade in amounts that are multiples of the standard lot size for the contract.

Currency Option: A contract that confers upon its buyer the right, but not the obligation, to enter into a foreign exchange contract at a particular price and date in the future for a price known as the premium. Such options are usually specified by their currency pair, strike price, expiration date, direction and amount. Most currency options traded are customized contracts dealt in the over-the-counter forex market, although standardized forex options also trade on the Chicago IMM and Philadelphia Stock Exchanges.

Currency Swap: A transaction involving selling or buying a certain amount of one currency pair for one date and simultaneously buying or selling that same amount for value on another date. The currency swap might also refer to the swap points that are the number of pips that need to be added or subtracted from the spot exchange rate to account for the cost of carry from spot value to the desired forward value date.

Currency: The primary unit of payment and hence the means by which trade occurs in a particular country. Physical currency can be made of either paper or coin, and it is usually issued by the country's government to serve as money within its borders.

Dealing Spread: The difference or spread between the immediate prices at which a dealer, broker or market maker is willing to buy and sell a particular commodity or other asset. The dealing spread is composed of a low bid price and a higher offer price which respectively represent where a market maker is willing to buy and sell the asset.

Discount Broker: A stockbroker that typically fills customer orders for a discounted commission but that does not provide stock market research or investment advice. A full-service stockbroker generally offers their clientele personal consultations, research, and tax and estate planning advice for the higher commissions they charge.

Dividend: A distribution of cash or other asset made by a company to the company's shareholders. The dividend amount or terms is typically decided on by the company's board of directors and the distribution can be made up of cash, shares of stock or other company property.

Earnings per Share: A portion of a company's after-tax earnings allocated to each share of the company's outstanding common stock. The Earnings per Share or EPS is an important indicator of a company's profitability and is calculated by taking the company's net income and dividing the amount by the number of outstanding shares. If the company has preferred stock then those dividends are discounted from net income.

Equities: Refers to the ownership interest of a company represented by shares of stock issued by that company. Equities make up the principal source of corporate financing in capitalist economies.

Equity Market: Refers to a system for trading stocks, which represent equity or ownership in the issuing corporations. Stocks are traded in the Equity Market on centralized and non-centralized stock exchanges, as well as over the counter.

Exchange Rate: The exchange rate or rate of exchange is the market-determined amount of the base or primary currency expressed in units of the counter or secondary currency. Typically, an exchange rate would be quoted for delivery in two business days or value spot.

Foreign Exchange Market: The forum in which participants buy and sell currencies against each other. Participants include central banks, commercial and investment banks, corporations, fund managers, hedge funds and personal forex traders.

Foreign Exchange Option: A contract that confers upon its buyer the right, but not the obligation, to enter into a foreign exchange contract at a particular price and date in the future for a price known as the premium. They are usually specified by their currency pair, strike price, expiration date, direction and amount. Most currency options traded are customized contracts dealt in the over-the-counter forex market, although standardized forex options trade on the Chicago IMM and Philadelphia Stock Exchanges.

Foreign Exchange Risk: The chance that fluctuations in currency exchange rates will adversely affect the value of an investment or contractual transaction. It can also refer to the possibility that a forex trader may have to take a loss on a trading position due to an unfavorable exchange rate movement.

Foreign Exchange: A transaction whereby the currency of one country is exchanged or traded for the currency of another country. Typically, this foreign exchange trade is done at a particular rate and for value "spot" or delivery of the two currencies in two business days, except for USD/CAD which typically delivers in just one business day.

Forex: A shortened form of the phrase "foreign exchange" that refers to transactions whereby the currency of one country is exchanged or traded for the currency of another country. Typically, this trade will be done at a particular rate of exchange and for value "spot" which is delivery of the two currencies in two business days, except for USD/CAD which typically delivers in just one business day.

Fundamental Analysis: A method of research that involves determining a commodity or other asset's intrinsic value by investigating the related financial and economic factors that influence its valuation. These factors could be related to the supply, demand, production and company's management, macro or microeconomic data and would determine if the security or asset is fairly valued, undervalued or overvalued.

Futures Contract: A standardized and transferable agreement traded on an exchange the price of which depends on that of an underlying asset. The delivery dates for such futures contracts will generally fall on a particular set of dates, often quarterly, in order to provide greater liquidity. Futures trade in amounts that are multiples of the standard lot size for the contract.

Futures Market: Refers to a system for trading futures contracts, which are agreements to transact a certain amount of a commodity on a future date. Futures markets consist of centralized exchanges located in various countries that are part of the overall commodities market.

Initial Public Offering: The first issuance of stock from a private company making the company publicly traded on a stock exchange or over-the-counter network. Initial public offerings are generally made by new companies hoping to raise more capital for expansion; however, large private companies also offer stock to become publicly traded. A company generally has to find an underwriter, which consists of an investment banker that is willing to purchase a percentage of the stock and is responsible for determining the type of security to offer, its valuation and initial distribution. Many initial public offerings have more than one underwriter.

Insider: A senior officer or director of a corporation or any person or entity that holds more than ten percent of a company's voting shares of stock. For the purpose of insider trading, an insider can be anyone who trades shares of a company's stock based on information not readily available to the public. Insiders must comply with disclosure requirements when they make purchases or sales of their equity holdings.

Interest Rate Parity: the theoretical relationship between the spot exchange rate, the forward rate and the interest rate differential between the two currencies involved in a particular currency pair. Basically, Interest Rate Parity requires that the interest rate differential equals the difference between the forward and spot rates.

Leverage: In finance, leverage is the use of debt for the financing of an activity. For example, an individual paying for a property with a mortgage or a company that has more than 80 percent debt relative to its assets would be considered leveraged. In commodities trading, leverage is achieved by using margin, which calls for a fraction of funds to be deposited in a margin account in order to control the purchase or short sale of securities.

Margin: A collateral amount used in the purchase or sale of futures contracts or CFDs. The margin for a purchase consists of the collateral amount that the buyer of the instrument needs to put up with the broker to cover the amount of risk of the transaction. For example, for the purchase of Heating Oil futures contracts worth $100,000, a margin deposit of 20 percent of the total notional amount or $20,000 is required by the broker or exchange to make the purchase.

Market Capitalization: The value of a company according to the total dollar value of the company's outstanding shares of stock. Also referred to as a company's "market cap", market capitalization is calculated by multiplying the total number of company shares outstanding by the market price of one share of the company's stock. For example, a company with 10 million shares outstanding and their common shares were trading at $10 apiece, would have a market cap of $100 million.

Market Close: The end of a trading session for any particular market. For example, the market close of the Chicago Mercantile Exchange occurs each weekday at 5:00PM Eastern Standard Time. A closed market refers to exchange holidays when no trading takes place.

Market Index: A market metric that consists of the weighted values of components included in a particular list of companies. A stock market index shows the performance of a group of component stocks weighted according to their shares outstanding and share price in a mathematical formula, for example the Dow Jones Industrial Average, an index which shows the performance of the 30 top U.S. industrial stocks.

Market Maker: An individual who makes two way prices on certain commodities, usually to clients or on exchanges. They may also watch and execute orders for clients.

Over-the-Counter or OTC: Refers to a decentralized market in which assets or financial instruments are not traded on an official exchange. In general, such OTC instruments will instead be dealt directly between counterparties over the telephone or via some other reliable means of communicating contractual terms, like an electronic dealing system for example.

Precious Metals: Metallic substances that have a high intrinsic economic value. Such metals are rare and serve as a store of intrinsic wealth for nations and individuals, as well as having various industrial applications. Precious metals include: gold, silver, palladium and platinum. They are traded on many of the world's largest commodity exchanges, such as the New York Mercantile Exchange, the London Metals Exchange and the Chicago Mercantile Exchange.

Price to Equity Ratio: The ratio of the book value of a common share of a company's stock to the stock's prevailing market price. The book value of equity is a measure of the shareholder's ownership equity based on the net worth of the company's assets. Therefore, if a stock is trading at $10 per share and the book value of the company is $5 per share, then the Price to Equity ratio would be 2.

Primary Market: The first market where securities are made available through an underwriter. They are traded on the Primary Market before being traded on an exchange or over-the-counter.

Range: A set of market prices bounded on the top by the high price and on the bottom by the low price of a futures contract or other asset observed during a particular trading time frame. For example, if WTI Crude Oil had a daily high of $60 per barrel and a daily low of $55 per barrel, then the range of that contract during the trading day was $55-$60.

Relative Purchasing Power Parity (Relative PPP): A theory that relates the change in the exchange rate between the currencies of two countries to their relative inflation rates. Specifically, Relative PPP equates the ideal spot exchange rate to the ratio of the cost of a good the first economy (expressed in currency one) to the cost of that same good in the second economy (expressed in currency two).

Retail Foreign Exchange Broker: A financial intermediary that generally caters to individual foreign exchange traders that typically trade currencies in smaller amounts for speculative purposes. Often such brokers offer online trading capabilities and many support automated forex trading.

Retail Forex: A term generally pertaining to individual foreign exchange traders that typically trade currencies in smaller amounts. Such smaller traders will often use technical analysis-based trading methods, and they generally trade forex for speculative purposes.

Resistance: A technical term that refers to an excess of supply of a commodity at a given price level. For example, if a commodity futures contract trades up to $12 per lot after opening at $10, and then trades back to $10, then the resistance level for that particular time frame would be at the $12 price the market reversed at.

Risk Aversion: A market reaction where an investor is exposed to uncertainty and makes investment decisions that tend to mitigate that uncertainty. For example, a risk averse investor might prefer to buy low-yielding U.S. Treasury Notes instead of taking more risk and purchasing a stock that might have a higher expected returns.

Secondary Market: The market in which securities are freely traded by all market participants. Examples of a Secondary Market include the stock and bond exchanges, commodities futures exchanges and the foreign exchange market.

Securities: Investment instruments of any kind, some of which represent ownership in corporations like stocks, and that are generally traded on secondary markets. Securities include: stocks and bonds, futures contracts, mutual funds and options.

Share Market: The stock or equity market which consists of a system for trading stocks. Stocks represent equity or ownership in the issuing corporations. Stocks are traded on centralized and non-centralized stock exchanges around the world that form the global Share Market.

Share: A single unit of stock ownership in a company. In generally, one Share of stock represents a proportional claim on a company's ownership, its assets and its profits relative to the total amount of shares issued by that company.

Stock Dividend: Refers to a dividend paid out to shareholders in shares of stock instead of cash. A Stock Dividend will generally be paid out in proportion to the amount of stock owned by the stockholder. A stock's dividend, on the other hand, is generally paid out to shareholders in cash.

Stock Market: Refers to a system for trading stocks, which represent equity or ownership in their issuing corporations. Stocks are traded on centralized and non-centralized stock exchanges that form a part of the overall Stock Market.

Stock Quote: An indication of the market price for the particular stock that the price is being obtained for. A Stock Quote typically comes with a bid price and an offer price, with the difference known as the spread.

Stock Symbol: The acronym assigned to a company's stock under which their stock is traded on an exchange. Symbols for New York and American Stock Exchange stocks consist of three letters, while stocks listed on the

Nasdaq market have four letters.

Stock: Refers to the shares of a corporation which represent an ownership interest in that corporation. Stocks can be issued privately or can be offered to the public and traded on an exchange.

Stockbroker: A legally registered representative that executes buy and sell orders for equities on behalf of their clients. A stockbroker can be either a full service broker or a discount broker. Full service brokers provide their customers with advice, research and other amenities, whereas discount brokers provide only brokering services with no extras.

Support: A technical analysis term that refers to an abundance of buy orders at a certain price level in a commodity or other asset. When its price reaches a level of support, the asset tends to move higher until reaching a level, known as resistance, where an excess of supply puts downward pressure on its price.

Technical Analysis: A method of investigation into the price patterns of commodities or other assets that depends on the levels of supply and demand. Technical analysis indicates at what prices assets are most likely to appreciate or decline by using indicators such as oscillators, moving averages and volume figures.

Trend: The prevailing direction of asset prices. For example, an upward trend would indicate that the price of a commodity is gaining, while a downward trend would indicate that its price is falling. Three major trends types can be discerned in an asset market: rising, declining and flat.

INDEX

Acquisitions, 24, 25
ADP Non-farm Employment Change, 59
Aggressor company, 28
Agricultural Commodities, 39
Balance Sheet, 15, 77
Building Permits, 55
Capacity Utilization Rate, 48
Capital Markets, 77
Capitalization, 19
Carry trades, 10
Carrying costs, 42
Cash Dividends, 29
Centralized stock exchange, 17
Closing Price, 77
Commitment of Traders, 6, 38
Commodity Valuation, 45
Consumer Confidence Index, 49
Consumer Price Index, 6, 38, 51
Corporation, 16, 77
CPI. *See* Consumer Price Index
Crack Spread, 42
Cross Rate, 77
Currency, 7, 8, 36, 77, 78
Currency Futures, 77
Currency Option, 10, 78
Currency Reserves, 8

Currency Swap, 78
Currency Valuation, 7
Dealing Spread, 78
Debt, 19
Discount Broker, 78
Diversification, 18
Dividend, 22, 28, 78
Earnings, 19
Earnings per Share, 20, 79
Economic Data, 5, 37
Economic indicators, 1, 47
Edwin Lefevre, 70
Employment Data, 6, 38
Enterprise Value, 21
Equities, 79
Equity Market, 79
Exchange Rate, 79
Existing Home Sales, 55
Fair Value, 20
Fed's Beige Book, 52
Forecasting, 23
Foreign Exchange, 79, 80, 83
Foreign Exchange Market, 79
Foreign Exchange Option, 79
Foreign Exchange Risk, 79
Forex, 6, 80, 83
Forex trading, 5

Fundamental analysis, 1, 2, 5, 15, 33, 37, 80
Fundamental Data, 37
Fundamentals, 6, 44
Further reading, 69
Futures Contract, 80
Futures Market, 80
Gambling, 1
GDP. *See* Gross Domestic Product
Geopolitical events, 6, 38
Greenmail, 27
Gross Domestic Product, 6, 38, 54
Growth, 24
Growth Rate, 20
Hostile Takeovers, 26
House Price Index, 55
Housing market, 55
Housing Starts, 55
HPI. *See* House Price Index
Industrial Production, 6, 38, 57
Inflation, 45
Initial Public Offering, 21, 80
Insider, 19, 81
Interest rate differential, 10
Interest rate parity, 9, 10
Interest rates, 6, 9
Investing, 17
Investment banks, 79
IPO. *See* Initial Public Offering
Issuing of stock, 16
Jack Schwager, 70
Jellyhawk Financial Press, ii, xi, 2, 71
Jobless Claims, 58
John G. Murphy, 71
Law of One Price, 13
Leverage, 81
Margin, 81
Market Capitalization, 20, 81
Market Close, 82
Market Index, 82

Market-makers, 4
Mergers, 24, 25
MetaTrader, ix
Michael Covel, 70
Microsoft, 18
New Home Sales, 55
New York Institute of Finance, 71
News, 4
News wire, 47
NFP. *See* Non-Farm Payrolls
Non-Farm Payrolls, 59
OTC. *See* Over-the-Counter
Over-the-Counter, 82
PCE. *See* Personal Consumption Expenditure
PEG. *See* Price Earnings to Growth Ratio
Pending Home Sales, 55
Personal Consumption Expenditure, 61
PMI. *See* Purchasing Manager's Index
Poison Pills, 27
Political Events, 40
PPI. *See* Producer Price Index
PPP. *See* Purchasing Power Parity
Precious Metals, 82
Price Earnings to Growth Ratio, 20
Price Factors, 40
Price to Equity Ratio, 82
Price to Sales Ratio, 21
Price/Earnings Ratio, 20
Primary Market, 83
Producer Price Index, 6, 38, 62
Purchasing Manager's Index, 64
Purchasing Power Parity, 12, 13, 83
Range, 83
Rate of return, 18
Relative Purchasing Power Parity, 83

Resistance, 83
Retail Foreign Exchange, 83
Retail Forex, 83
Retail Sales, 6, 38, 65
Return on Assets, 21
Return on Investment Capital, 21
Revenue, 23
Reverse Stock Splits, 31
Risk Aversion, 83
ROA. *See* Return on Assets
ROIC. *See* Return on Investment Capital
Secondary Market, 84
Securities, 84
Share, 84
Share Market, 84
Soybean Complex, 43
Specialist, 82
Spread positions, 33
Spreads, 43

Stock, 85
Stock Dividends, 29, 84
Stock Market, 84
Stock of a Nation, 7
Stock Quote, 84
Stock splits, 30
Stock Symbol, 84
Stockbroker, 85
Supply and demand, 6, 38
Supply and Demand, 35
Support, 85
Synergy, 26
Target Company, 27
Technical Analysis, 1, 70, 71, 85
TheFXperts, 74
Trade Balance, 6, 38, 66
Trade Forex, 6
Trend, 85
Unemployment Rate, 59
Weather, 35, 38

www.ingramcontent.com/pod-product-compliance
Lightning Source LLC
Chambersburg PA
CBHW020448220526
45464CB00002B/908